DOWNBOUND

FROM JAYBIRD ON THE LITTLE PIGEON RIVER TO CHAIRMAN OF THE TENNESSEE VALLEY AUTHORITY

THE MEMOIRS OF
John B. Waters, Jr.

THE NEXUS COMPANY LLC
119 Commerce Street
Sevierville, TN 37862-3524

Copyright 2000 by John B. Waters, Jr.

DOWNBOUND

*FROM JAYBIRD ON THE LITTLE
PIGEON RIVER TO CHAIRMAN OF THE
TENNESSEE VALLEY AUTHORITY*

THE MEMOIRS OF
John B. Waters, Jr.

Copyright 2000 by John B Waters, Jr. All rights are reserved.

Publisher
The Nexus Company, LLC
119 Commerce Street
Sevierville, Tennessee 37862-3524
(865) 453-1051

SAN 253-2581
Library of Congress Number 00-132898
ISBN 0-9700926-0-1

Printed by Vaughan Printing of Nashville, TN, in the United States of America.

Cover Design - LaPrees Advertising and Design of Sevierville, TN.

Computer Typesetting by Douglas Graphics, Sevierville, TN.

DOWNBOUND

FROM JAYBIRD ON THE LITTLE PIGEON RIVER TO CHAIRMAN OF THE TENNESSEE VALLEY AUTHORITY

THE MEMOIRS OF
John B. Waters, Jr.

CONTENTS

1. Acknowledgements 11
2. Prologue 13
3. The Early Years 16
4. World War II 23
5. School 25
6. Interesting People 31
7. Doctors, Drug Stores, Mills and Theatres 39
8. Jobs 48
9. Life In Sevierville 58
10. Dinner Is At Noon 63
11. Monday Is Wash Day 69
12. When Winter Came 71
13. Cars 73
14. The Sevier County Fair 79
15. The Connection 85
16. The Navy 99
17. Politics 112
18. Lawyering 121
19. Smoky Mountain Queen 142
20. Appalachian Regional Commission 158
21. Tennessee Valley Authority 171
22. Voyage For The Valley 184
23. I Am A Baptist 206

DOWNBOUND

On the river the boatman is either UPBOUND or DOWNBOUND. The current is DOWNBOUND and in general gives the boatman less control than the UPBOUND boat he meets. For this reason the old rule was that the DOWNBOUND boat has the right of way. Sevier County is home of the Great Smoky Mountains with the high peaks of LeConte and Clingman's Dome. From Sevierville it's all DOWNBOUND.

JBW

To Patsy

Who Makes It All Worthwhile

ACKNOWLEDGEMENTS

Relatives, friends, business and professional associates have all contributed to this book either directly or indirectly. They are the players in the events I have described. It has been my good fortune to be surrounded by good people during the time I grew up in Sevierville and later as a lawyer and in the activities with which I have been involved. It seems that I have always had around me good people, people with ability, men and women of character who were motivated to do a good job, people who were always willing to help me along in life and my own undertakings. It seems that these people realized I needed help and were willing to help me. From that I have benefited and I am indeed grateful.

The secretaries that have been in my employment are a good example. My first secretary after I was licensed to practice law was Mary Fine Rolan. Mary is now deceased. She was not an experienced secretary and I was not an experienced lawyer. So we both learned together and she gave me excellent service.

When I went to the Appalachian Regional Commission in Washington I was very fortunate to hire a secretary who had a tremendous knowledge of the federal government. She had worked in the OMB (Office of Management and Budget). I hired her and brought her to the Appalachian Regional Commission. Her name was Vivian Thompson, a beautiful African-American lady who served me extremely well and kept me out of a lot of difficulty. Vivian always seemed to be ahead of me whenever there was something I needed to be doing. She generally knew what needed to be done before it occurred to me.

When I returned to Sevierville and got back into the practice of law I was very fortunate to have Barbara (Bobby) Myers as my secretary. Barbara is a brilliant lady. She gained an excellent knowledge of the law and the clients we represented. Barbara had a remarkable memory for things we had done in the past.

When I went to the Tennessee Valley Authority I was again blessed by working with Cathy Wallace Hutchins. She had an in-depth knowledge of TVA. Cathy was very loyal to me and had a unique ability to coordinate my schedule and keep up with an awful lot of appointments and travel and people that I needed to see, as well as keeping me straight as to who people were in TVA, which was a very big organization. She made my job more efficient and very pleasurable. When I became chairman Gail Kitts joined Cathy and I and was a big help.

After I returned to Sevierville I hired Jackie Turner as my secretary. Jackie typed and retyped this manuscript and did an excellent job in helping with the preparation of the book in general.

I am indebted to all these ladies because they were all bright and possessed a lot of ability and were well motivated and loyal to me, willing to help me in whatever task we had before us as a particular time. I was truly blessed to have this kind of assistance.

Gary Hunt was hired by the Tennessee Bar Association about the time I became president. Gary, I quickly realized, had a lot of skills in writing and gathering information and getting it down in a way that somebody could read and understand it. Gary has helped in the editing of this book immeasurably and I am indeed grateful to him.

Anna Garber of Sevierville and Amanda Kinard of Nashville read the manuscript and made grammar, spelling and sentence construction corrections.

Many of the pictures are by my daughter Cyndy and Bob Kollar of TVA. My nephew, David Paine Waters, scanned the pictures for the book and put them on a CD.

PROLOGUE

My home town is Sevierville, Tennessee. This little town was first known as Forks of the River before it was named for John Sevier, Tennessee's first governor. The Little Pigeon River begins in Sevier County in the Great Smoky Mountains. The west fork is made up of small creeks and branches falling from Newfound Gap and Mount LeConte. From the North Carolina line at Newfound Gap it is 15.7 miles to Gatlinburg. Over this distance the streams fall about 3,700 feet. Over another 13 miles and a drop of 400 feet, the river picks up more creeks and branches and gets to Sevierville. The east fork is very similar except it comes out of the mountains above Pittman Center. The two forks meet at Sevierville. It is difficult to do much boating above Sevierville except in high water, and the river is not very deep even at Sevierville.

As a boy my friends and I would swim in the Sheppard Hole on the west fork or in the Reno hole on the east fork. Occasionally the Sheppard Hole would have a place over my head.

One summer day a number of us boys were in the Reno Hole. No one had a bathing suit and all were swimming "jaybird". A father and his son, a boy about our age, came walking across the swinging bridge to the right bank.

"He wants to go swimming with you boys," the boy's Daddy said, "but watch out for him ... He can't swim."

"Don't worry, Mr. Cooper," Jack Snapp said. "It's just peter deep."

Mr. Scarlett, a farmer who lived near the Reno Hole, would occasionally run us off from the swimming hole. He didn't like us going in there jaybird. He would come to the left bank and holler at us, "You boys get out of there.

The very idea ... in the river showing your secrets!"

I was fascinated to learn that 50 years before that time many flatboats, loaded with Sevier County produce, went down the river — some all the way to New Orleans. My daddy also told me that a lot of our topsoil had gone to the Gulf of Mexico and was building up the State of Louisiana. This hardly seemed fair to me and I wondered if Daddy was right about that.

As you can see, at Sevierville the only way you can go on the river is downstream.

I fell in love with the river. I love to be on the river or just sitting on the bank watching the river meander by. Today my home, Water's Edge, is on a small bluff, 55 feet above the Reno Hole.

Legend has it that the Indians believed the valley belongs to the river. The Indian was right. It is a place of relaxation. It is exciting to hear the roar of the shoals and rapids. The slow pools and eddies whisper of romance.

AND SO ... Let's go with the river — relax. We're Down Bound.

107 Joy Street, Sevierville, Tennessee...JBW birthplace

JBW, age 6

JBW, School Days

THE EARLY YEARS

I was born on Joy Street in Sevierville, about half a block from the Sevier County Courthouse and only a block from the railroad trestle that crossed the West Prong of the Little Pigeon. Somewhat upstream from that point, about a block and a half from my home, was the swinging bridge that went across the West Prong near the McMahan Indian Mound.

At a very early age I discovered the river and I have been fascinated by rivers ever since. I recall asking my father where the water from the Little Pigeon River went. He explained that five miles below Sevierville the Little Pigeon River emptied into the French Broad. At Knoxville the French Broad joined the Holston to became the Tennessee River, and then the Tennessee emptied into the Ohio and then the Mississippi and finally into the Gulf of Mexico below New Orleans. This provided a lot of thought for my young mind and my imagination followed the river and to all the great interconnected oceans of the world.

As a young lad I just liked to be on the river. I ran up and down the banks and fished some, but mostly I just liked to be on the river. By the of age 12 I wanted very badly to acquire a flat-bottomed boat, the kind of boat that was common on the rivers around Sevierville. They were 12, 14 or 16 feet long, a couple of feet wide at the beam and had two blunt ends. They were floored with lumber running across the sides of the boat. A number of carpenters made these boats. They were not very complicated boats to make.

On the East Prong of the Little Pigeon River just above the Mill Dam lived a man named Frank Wynn. Frank was a very interesting person to me. He was very small with dark olive skin. A good craftsman and carpenter, his main interests in life were hunting and fishing. He particularly loved to fish the river. He and his wife lived in a little house right on the riverbank. His wife worked for a very prominent banker in town, and I suppose she basically supported the family.

Frank was a good boat builder. It was not unusual, especially in the spring, for him to be in his back yard there on the bank of the Little Pigeon River building boats. So I entered into negotiations with Frank for a boat. At the time $14 was an average price for a boat, the price varying with the length of boat required. I didn't have $14 so I talked to Frank about how I could get a boat. He agreed to build me a boat for $8, if I would furnish the paint and paint it and get my own chain. You had to have a chain on the front end of your boat to secure it to a good sycamore tree on the bank of the river. These boats were too heavy to move in and out of the water too often. I wanted to put my boat at the swinging bridge on the West Prong, and it was not unusual for there to be four or five boats chained to the couple of sycamores that were located there. Frank suggested I might find a chain in my father's barn, which was across the river not too far from where Frank lived. "I bet you can find you a chain there," he said, " and that'll save you a couple of dollars. So if you do that and do your own paint, you can have this boat for $8."

So we made a deal.

Every year my mother painted some very fine wicker furniture that sat on the front porch of our home. This wicker furniture was always green. She always did this painting herself out in the yard using papers and gloves and rags. So, as you might guess, my boat ended up green.

After I got the boat built I put it in the water there at Frank's. You had to put these boats in the water and leave for them a few days because the bottom had to swell tight. Frank did not fit the boards up tight against each other, but used a 20-penny nail as the measure of the crack he left between boards. Then he would put the boat in the water and in a few days it would swell tight and then you would bail it out. You moved the boat with homemade paddles. I can't remember ever seeing a factory-made boat paddle; we made them as best as we could — homemade. You also had a pole about 10 feet long because the depth of the Little Pigeon was such you could pole your boat.

After I got my boat watertight and ready to go at Frank's, I went down to the Mill Dam. Of course, I had to take it over the dam, but that was no big test, and I went down a very short distance and hung a left, coming up the West Prong of the Little Pigeon to where I wanted to keep my boat at the swinging bridge.

I enjoyed that boat very much the next couple of years. It was a big part of my life. I spent a lot of time on the river and had a couple of trot lines that I ran. I also acquired another very prized possession, a single-shot Remington 22 bolt-action rifle. I bought this at Robertson Brothers and Sharp's Hardware for $5.95. So with my boat and my 22 rifle I spent many, many happy hours as a young boy on the Little Pigeon River around Sevierville. I became a pretty good shot and I really learned to love just being on the river.

In 1941 I was twelve years old and World War II had commenced. Also, construction of Douglas Dam had begun. This was a tremendous happening in Sevier County and a subject of considerable debate. As a matter of fact it was debated very hotly in my family. My father was very much in favor of the dam. He believed that the dam would bring a measure of economic progress to Sevier County and the surrounding area. He explained forcefully to me how important electricity was, although I had already learned that through my own observation.

On the other hand, my mother's father, a lawyer in Sevierville, opposed the dam. He felt like a dam on the French Broad would cover up some of the finest farmland in the world, that the land that would be covered up was simply too valuable and would be too great a loss and the dam shouldn't be built there. Certainly Douglas Dam did cover up some of the finest farmland in the world; but at any rate, I recall hearing this debated in the family circle. My father and grandfather were partners in real estate and other investments and got along really well, but their politics were certainly different. My grandfather was a Democrat, and his father had been a Confederate soldier. My father came from a long line of Republicans. I became a Republican because my father explained to me that when he and my mother got married they agreed she would handle the religious education in the family and he would handle the political education. So we all became Baptists and Republicans.

The building of Douglas Dam, which started in 1941, was certainly the most important thing that had happened in Sevier County since the Great Smoky Mountains National Park had been established. It was indeed a tremendous thing. It boggled the mind of a twelve-year-old boy to contemplate how this dam would back up water over all these thousands of acres and fit into the TVA plan for the valley. I really can't say that I understood a great deal of TVA's work at that point in time, but I saw first hand what a wonderful thing electricity is, and I saw TVA create jobs and create this lake. So I was very interested in the lake.

Under TVA's plan the lake was impounded. You couldn't fish in it for a year to give the fish stock time to mature and grow. So I was about fourteen years old when my brother David (who was four years older) and I began to go to Douglas Lake. What a tremendous thing to see a body of water this vast, this big. The summer before he went into the Army, David and I went to the lake almost every day. We had a boat out on the lake and we trolled, mostly catching bass. At night we would go frog hunting. I still kept the green boat on the Little Pigeon River and kept some trot lines there. It was a great way to spend a summer.

I never recall being afraid of the water, nor do I remember not knowing how to swim. There were no swimming pools in Sevierville, or anywhere else in Sevier County when I grew up, but you certainly needed to know how to swim on the lake. While the Little Pigeon water wasn't deep, not over your head in many places, the lake water was certainly over your head and many people who lived on the French Broad River were taught to be afraid of it. Many of my friends who lived there would not get out on the river at all. I was never taught to be afraid of the river and I'm grateful for that, but I was taught respect for the river, that it was a strong, living, vital force. As my Dad said, "The river's kind of like a mule. You can do things with it, but it can kick you too." You've got to learn to respect the river.

So my introduction to TVA was Douglas Dam. I did learn to respect TVA as well. I suppose as I grew older I lost some of my interest in TVA itself, but my father always told me that the people who live in Sevier County should respect and support three things: the Great Smoky Mountains National Park, the Tennessee Valley Authority and the University of Tennessee. So I was taught to respect TVA and later on I learned some of the history of TVA and became aware that TVA did do a great deal to drive economic development in the valley. I don't know that I understood economic development for some time, but I certainly saw improvements in agriculture, the use of fertilizer, putting electricity into rural homes and rural communities, and what it meant to Sevier County, because I'm old enough to remember times when rural sections didn't have electricity. I remember what a blessing electricity was and I always remember that old Baptist preacher who, after electricity came into his community, the next Sunday was preaching his sermon and said, "Brothers and Sisters, we all know that the greatest thing in the world is to have the love of God in your heart. But, brothers and sisters, let me tell you the second greatest thing is to have electricity in your home."

What a great thing electricity was, removing the burden of toil from the backs of men in farming work, and particularly from the women who lived in the valley. Electricity made their lives so much easier and gave them a quality of life that I don't think any other invention of man brought.

In 1984 I was given the opportunity to go on the TVA board. I talked about this decision with my friend Howard Baker, who was then the Majority Leader of the United States Senate. I told Howard I thought I would like to be on the board; and through his recommendation and influence, in August of 1984, I went on the board. Quite frankly, I saw myself reliving my childhood occupation of running up and down the river, this time the big Tennessee River.

A view of Sevierville showing the Little Pigeon River at the original forks, before the TVA flood control project.

JBW and Patsy at a formal dance during their years as students at the University of Tennessee.

WORLD WAR II

I was twelve years old when the United States entered World War II. When Japan attacked Pearl Harbor on December 7, 1941 I was in the seventh grade. At that time the seventh and eighth grades were in the Sevier County High School Building on High Street. Mr. Ledwell, the principal, had all the students, high school and seventh and eighth grades, go in the auditorium and hear President Franklin D. Roosevelt make his famous radio address declaring war on Germany and Japan. This was on Monday, December 8, 1941. It was one of those days I will always remember.

The Sevier County Draft Board was located in what is now the Ogle Building. When a group of men were drafted a bus would be chartered to take to them to Fort Oglethorpe, Georgia, for induction. At first there would be one bus parked on Court Avenue and about 5 p.m. the townspeople would come to see the men leave on the bus. Later I remember seeing buses lined up all the way to Joy Street. There was a lot of hugging, kissing and crying as sweethearts and family said good-bye to loved ones. I remember one prominent young man who had too much to drink announcing to all that he would take care of both Hitler and Tojo and the war would be over soon.

A story was told of one man who lived way back in the eastern part of the county near the Cocke County line. He had been sent his draft notice, but he did not want to go. He didn't show up at the draft board office. The "law" went to his house and told him the country was at war and a lot of men were being drafted into the army.

"What's this was all about?" he asked.

The officer told him about Adolph Hitler and all the bad things he was doing.

"Well, hell fire," the man replied. "You don't need to go to all this trouble for that. I could take care of that pretty easy!"

"How could you do that?" asked the officer.

"Well, you show me where he lives and I'll slip up there in the dark before daylight and when he comes out on the porch to piss in the morning, I'll shoot the SOB."

Several people thought that was a good idea, but they drafted him anyway.

Everyone was very patriotic. We had air raid drills where we would turn off all lights and the wardens (men too old to be drafted) would come around and see if the houses were properly blacked out.

Many things were rationed. The Sevier County Ration Board had an office at 103 Joy Street. Mr. George Allen and Mr. Lefford Sarten, two World War I veterans, ran the Ration Board. The people were issued "stamps" which permitted the purchase of the rationed items. Sugar, shoes, tires, gasoline and many other items were scarce and very limited. All new 1942 cars and trucks were confiscated and taken by the government. No new cars were sold to the public until 1946.

Every car had a two-inch sticker on the windshield. The car owner qualified for either an "A", "B", or "C" sticker. The "A" sticker was the general family car and received the lowest amount of stamps for gasoline. The "B" sticker was allowed more gasoline, and "C" the largest allocation, reserved for doctors and emergency vehicles.

Reports of deaths and injuries became frequent. The first one I remember, which got a lot of attention, was when Carl Rambo was wounded and received the Purple Heart medal. The medal was displayed in Rawlings Furniture Store window and people would congregate on the sidewalk and look at the medal. Unfortunately, Purple Hearts became more commonplace later.

SCHOOL

I started school at the age of six in 1935 at Sevierville Elementary School in Sevierville. The school was located in the old Murphy College building on Cedar Street. The building now houses the superintendent of schools offices. I walked to school. It was only about two blocks up Joy Street to Park Road, and then a back sidewalk led behind the Methodist Church and on the school property. Later I rode my bicycle.

Mr. Stanley Nave was principal, and Mrs. Pern Price was my first teacher. I did not learn much my first year. Mother said I learned to spell only two words: "all" and "tall." It was so bad that Mother got a few other parents together and organized a summer school with Mrs. Lewis Hamilton as teacher. My classmates were Bill Lee, Joe DeLozier, Bud Wilson, Jack Snapp, Sarah McAfee, Willie Kate Allen and Vivian Robertson.

The economy was bad during those first school years. Many of the students were poorly clothed and I am sure that some were poorly fed. I always went home for lunch, as there was no cafeteria. There was very little activity other than classwork. Roller skating and some basketball were popular. Shooting marbles and spinning tops added some sport to our day. I took voice lessons and sang at many school events and chapel programs.

After school when I came home Mother always had something for me to eat as I read the funnies in the newspapers. The boys played "cowboy," "kick the can," or "hide and seek."

In 1940 I "graduated" from the sixth grade and left the elementary school for the seventh and eighth grades. I still walked or rode my bicycle home for lunch. After school my friends and I, along with many other young people, headed for Lee's Drug Store on Court Avenue. The Park Theater had good movies and we saw almost all of them. Douglas Dam was under construction by TVA, and new people moved to Sevierville, including many new children. There were few houses and apartments available for the TVA people and some had to take rooms in private homes. We were curious about the building of the dam. We heard stories of families who had to sell their farms for the project. It did bring a better economy for Sevierville. The dam was built in thirteen months, and then the families were gone. I later learned that Douglas Dam was built with a twenty-four-hour work crew to furnish power to the new town of Oak Ridge in Anderson County. The Manhattan Project, the building of the atomic bomb, was a secret project of our government at Oak Ridge. Its use resulted in the ending of the war with Germany and Japan in later years.

About this time I discovered girls and I was at one time or another in love with almost every girl of my acquaintance. I discovered that Sevierville had a number of absolutely beautiful girls living right around town. Much later I learned that out in the county and the rural areas this number was multiplied many, many times.

The first ones I noticed, that suddenly took on a new and different interest to me, were the ones around town that I had grown up and always been friends with. We always had a crowd that ran together, mostly from my class. There was Willie Kate Allen, who was in our church and had always been a very close friend, now Mrs. Chandler McMahan. And there was Vivian Robertson, now Mrs. Jim Miner; Sarah McAfee, now Mrs. Ed Collins; and Carolyn Atchley, now Marshall. These girls were in my class and were always very close friends, and at one time or another I suppose I dated every one of them.

There was another group of girls that I always enjoyed being around, mostly in the class behind me. This included Betty Jo Ogle, now Burgin; Mary Lynn (Swan) Allen; Mary Alice Dennis, now Teague; Martha Lee Rawlings, now Hill; and Jackie Seaton, now Randles. Added to that group was Charlotte Atchley, Carolyn's sister, and Dorothy Lewallen, later Mrs. Dennis Mize. This was kind of our crowd and we ran together as good friends before dating started. At one time or another I was probably in love with every one of them.

Of course, a very special girl lived on Court Avenue, just a few doors down from Joy Street. This was Patsy Temple. Patsy and I have now completed forty-seven years of being together. She has stood by me every step of the way. We've had a wonderful life together.

We went to the little parties that young children go to and later we went to the parties of teenagers. The war was going on most of that time so there was not a lot that went on at school, but sometimes the schools had plays and programs, as well as sporting events that brought us together in games. We also had church events and we didn't limit ourselves to just one church. We went wherever there was something going on, whether it was at a Methodist, Presbyterian or Baptist church.

We really loved to dance. Mrs. Fred Atchley would allow us to dance in their apartment over Atchley's Supermarket down on the square. We spent many evenings there dancing to phonograph records. We could also dance in the Pines Theatre, especially on Sunday afternoon, with the good sound system there.

Other group activities included trips to the Great Smoky Mountains National Park, especially picnics at the Chimney Campgrounds area and other locations. Of course, we all loved going swimming at Pine Grove, and a trip to Knoxville to see a movie was very special and a good activity for dates when we got a little older.

Roller skating was a big thing to do when I was a small boy. There were a lot of sidewalks in the town and we could roller skate on the sidewalks. The old Methodist Community Building, which had been a gymnasium, was nearly rotted down. One end of the floor had actually sunk, but it still made a really good place to roller skate. Later Mr. Nave allowed us to skate on the floor of the gym in the elementary school as well. I thought it was a real treat to hold hands with a pretty girl and skate around the rink.

The headquarters of all youth, from young children to teenagers, was Lee's Drugstore. Dr. Lee was the owner-pharmacist there and the father of Bill Lee, my very close personal friend. Dr. Lee loved young people. The drugstore had a soda fountain, as most drugstores did back then. It was a real treat to go in and buy a soda or Coca-Cola or ice cream. When school was out that was where the young people congregated. They sat in there and read Doc's magazines while Doc played by ear on an old piano he kept in there. He really put up with us kids and we all loved him. He was a very special part of growing up. Doc Lee set an example for us, without lecturing or anything like that. I always thought it was kind of unusual that he would allow a child to run an account at the soda fountain. He would allow charges up to fifty or sixty cents and I often wondered how many he never collected.

I started at the University of Tennessee in Knoxville in 1947 and I'm afraid that I was poorly prepared for college. I had not applied myself in high school and I had not learned how to study or earn good grades. I have blamed World War II and the unsettled times of my high school years, but I know that I did not appreciate the importance of education during those years. The University of Tennessee brought me to a rather abrupt understanding. UT was filled with returning war veterans. The campus was overcrowded. Temporary classrooms were constructed like barracks over The Hill. Housing was scarce. There were no men's dormitories then. It took me a year to decide that I had to settle down, get to work, or drop out.

Several of my friends transferred to smaller schools, where they thought it might be easier. I considered a transfer, but decided I would go to work and make the grade. I did this with a lot of help. My fraternity, Phi Sigma Kappa, aided and encouraged me. My big brother, Joe Rogoski, was a very important help to me. I learned that attending class and paying attention was the best way for me to learn. It was popular and very cool to cut class. In most instances the teacher did not care and some students could "cram" for the finals and make a passing, or better, grade. This did not work for me. I had to get a good night's sleep before a final and get up in time to eat a good breakfast if I was to do well on a final exam. Even after I learned how to be a "good" student, I was never an "excellent" student.

My years at the University of Tennessee were truly great years, both for me and certainly for the university. World War II was over. Many returning veterans were there. The school had almost doubled in size from about four thousand students before World War II to up to seven or eight thousand immediately after. This caused problems at the university. A lot of temporary barracks had to be set up for housing and were even brought in for classrooms. They were scattered all over the hill. It made a fairly unsightly campus, but still it served until permanent facilities could be erected.

Due to my participation in campus politics, I was fortunate to be vice president of the student body and a member of the Athletic Council. Two students were elected to the Athletic Council, but they shared only one vote. The council was the governing body for the UT total athletic program.

Flemming Reeder and I were the two students. It was a great year, Tennessee had a fantastic football season, lost only to Mississippi State, and went on to win the Cotton Bowl in Dallas on January 1, 1951. It was, of course, a great time for our famous coach, General Neyland. Beating Texas twenty to fourteen in the Cotton Bowl this year was a highlight of his career. I was fortunate to know a number of the players and this was a fine team. They were not only good football players, but many were good students and in general just conducted themselves well and gave UT football players a good reputation on the campus.

Hank Lauricella was our All American and he played an outstanding game at the Cotton Bowl. Hank and Jim Haslam, also a member of the team, were good friends and we three were all majoring in finance. My fraternity brother, Andy Kozar, shared the high honors with Lauricella in the Cotton Bowl game. Another fraternity brother, Murphy Miller, and I went to Dallas. A train called the Cotton Bowl Special left Knoxville and went to Dallas and we went on the train. The 1951 Cotton Bowl was a fantastic event to attend as a UT student.

The Cotton Bowl game got started off with a lead for Tennessee when Hank Lauricella tossed to Vince Kaseta, another of my fraternity brothers, for twenty-seven yards and they added a field goal to the score.

After we returned from Dallas the Athletic Council met. General Neyland had been receiving a salary of fifteen thousand dollars a year as Vol coach and due to the good season and victory in Dallas, the Athletic Department had made plenty of money. We raised his salary to twenty-five thousand dollars after that game.

Tennessee became the National Champions for 1951, certainly a high honor for General Neyland and the football team. The team was recognized with the presentation of the national intercollegiate football trophy, which Notre Dame had won the previous year. We waited until 1998 to win the national championship again.

A fantastic team returned for 1952, including Ted Daffer, Hank Lauricella and Bill Pearman, who were named All-Americans. A number of other teammates were honored very highly. Tennessee was undefeated that year and went to the Sugar Bowl in New Orleans for the New Year's Day game, playing the University of Maryland. This was a very special game for Hank Lauricella because he was returning to his home town to play. Unfortunately, the game resulted in a twenty-eight to thirteen victory for Maryland and a loss for Tennessee.

I really enjoyed the university. I was active in my fraternity and on the campus. I became what was called a BMOC, Big Man On Campus. I especially enjoyed the social life. During those years fraternities and sororities held formal dances, usually in the Alumni Gym. I had a tux, a white dinner jacket and "tails." Patsy and I began to date steadily at the end of her second year, and we were "pinned" during the last year.

The many friends Patsy and I made at UT have enhanced our lives. The university was a very important part of my life and I am very proud to be a graduate. For me the social, extra-curricular, and associations with other people were every bit as important as the academic part.

My return to the university for law school was a totally different world. I finally became a student in the true sense of the word.

INTERESTING PEOPLE

Sevierville has always had a number of interesting people who either lived in our community permanently or who visited here. Some came here for extended periods of time. As a young man I was aware of these people because I could see them. A number of them lived in the Central Hotel, which was down on the square, and in the boarding houses or apartment houses around the town, particularly the Wade Apartments which were on Joy Street just four doors up from where I lived at 107 Joy Street.

I remember one man in particular who came here during the summer, sometime prior to the start of World War II. He lived in the Wade Apartments and he primarily caught my attention because of his unusual dress. His dress could be described as outlandish by Sevierville's ordinary standards at that date. He wore a straw hat which I guess had been painted. It had some red and green on it. He also wore a very colorful coat that had some white and green and red and a very colorful shirt and tie, and he wore white trousers with white shoes. He was a very fair complexioned, red-faced man. Why he came to Sevierville, I have no idea, but I do know he was here at least one summer. I would see him as he walked down Joy Street from the Wade Apartments to downtown Sevierville, where he would eat his meals. Generally I think he always ate in the Dick Allen Cafe. He might have eaten occasionally in what was the Sandwich Shop, which was just down Bruce Street, or the American Cafe, which was on down Court Avenue. Those were the three major eating establishments in town at that time.

I used to see him walk down the street and primarily because of his dress my curiosity about this man got more intense. I asked my father who he was and Dad said he didn't know. My father had seen him in town. The man certainly called attention to himself because of his dress, and Dad said the story around town was that he was a Communist. Well, this further heightened my curiosity because I had no earthly idea what a Communist was. This was prior to World War II so Communism was not something generally talked about in the community at that point in time.

I specifically remember one evening after supper, but yet way prior to dark, he was seated over on one of the benches in the courthouse yard and I got up my nerve and said, "Uh, I'm Johnny Waters. I live on Joy Street and I see you walking down Joy Street coming downtown."

"Yes," he said, "I have seen you there in your yard."

"Well, uh," I said, "I'd just kind of like to know a little bit about who you are."

"Well," he answered, "I'm surprised that you would be interested in me. Why are you interested in me?"

"Just because I see you," I said, "and you dress a little differently from most of the men in town and you cause some talk about who you are around town."

He said, "Well, is that so? I'm certainly interested in that. What do they say about me?"

I said, "Well, I've heard that they say that you are a Communist, but I don't know what that is."

He says, "Well," he says, "you don't know then whether you're a Communist or not."

I said, "No, sir. No, sir, I don't."

"Well," he says, "what are you?"

I said, "Well, I don't know exactly what you mean, but I'm a Baptist and a Republican."

"Well, Johnny," he said, "in that event I can tell you that you are not a Communist."

So they called him Sunshine and after that summer Sunshine disappeared as mysteriously as he had appeared on the scene, and I never heard from him again. That was certainly my first experience with a Communist.

At about the same time as Sunshine came to town, another man came and opened a jewelry store or watchmaker's shop about in the middle of

Bruce Street, over on the north side of the street. It should be understood that anything new that happened in our town, a new business, a new building, was the subject of conversation because they were important events. Well, this man led to a lot of discussion in town because nobody knew who he was or where he came from. And the word circulated around town that he was a Jew. Well, we didn't have any Jewish people at all in the community that I knew, so several of us boys, Bill Lee and Joe DeLozier, Bud Wilson maybe, Jack Snapp and I, were sitting in the yard of a dwelling house across the road from the jewelry store and looking through the hedge, trying to get a view of this man. We wanted to see what a Jew looked like. I don't know why we assumed he might look differently, but anyway, that's what we were doing.

Mr. Ed Shepard, a very prominent merchant who owned a dry goods store, came by and saw us. He asked, "What are you boys doing sitting here?"

We said, "Well, we're looking across the street at that new jewelry store over there. We're trying to see that man. We want to see what he looks like."

"Well, why are you interested in him?"

"We've heard that he's a Jew and we want to see what a Jew looks like."

"Well," he said, "you're wasting your time. He's a Catholic."

So Mr. Shepard walked on up the street and we considered that remark. We decided we'd still better stay there and look because we didn't know what a Catholic looked like either.

Well, we never did see the man that day, but we found out later that it didn't make any difference. He was not a Jew. He was not a Catholic. He was a Seventh Day Adventist. But we didn't know what that was either. Our education about people was very limited at that time.

I mentioned Mr. Shepard previously. Mr. Shepard was an interesting man in his own right. As I said, he was a merchant, had a dry goods store, and was a prominent man. He always wore a three-piece suit with a vest. In his vest pocket, which you could see because I don't think he ever buttoned up his coat, you could see the double handles of a pair of scissors. I noticed that on more than one occasion and again young boy curiosity made me wonder why he would carry what was obviously a fairly small pair of scissors in his vest pocket.

So again I went to my source of information, my mother and daddy. I asked my daddy, "I see Mr. Shepard down there in town, Dad, and he has this pair of scissors in his vest pocket. Why would he carry them?"

My dad said, "Well, son, Mr. Shepard carries those scissors to clip the coupons on his bonds."

Well, that didn't cure my curiosity. It enhanced it. I had no earthly idea what he meant. But Dad explained to me that Mr. Shepard bought these bonds with little coupons on the bottom. That was the way those bonds paid their interest. He had a large number of these bonds, so he would go to the bank periodically, probably even once a week, get in his lock box and get out these bonds. Then he would clip the coupons off the bonds that had matured and the bank teller gave him money.

I thought that was an interesting way to make money and I told myself that I wanted to remember that. I guess, however, the day of bond coupons has passed. I don't know that any today even have coupons, but every time I saw Mr. Shepard I figured, well, he's been down and got his money clipping those coupons.

The Wade Apartments on Joy Street were owned by Mrs. Victoria Wade, a very prominent woman in Sevierville, who also owned and operated Wade's Department Store with her son, Dwight.

Living in the Wade Apartments was another woman named Helen Sharp. As far as I know, Helen Sharp was the only registered nurse in Sevier County during that period of time. She literally practiced medicine, taking her little black bag in her car all over the county to deliver babies and treat illness.

Her appearance always caught my attention because she wore the white uniform and white shoes and the cap of a registered nurse. She also wore a black cape that came below her waist and was lined in red. She was an interesting sight to see on the street, with the cape flaring in the breeze, a very distinguished looking person and highly admired for her medical ability.

Right across the street from the Wade Apartments lived Mrs. Ethel Chandler, also a woman of a lot of prominence in the town. She was the secretary to my grandfather, Judge A. M. Paine. We youngsters were always amused in the late evening to see Mrs. Helen Sharp cross the street from the Wade Apartments to go to over to Mrs. Chandler's house to have their evening toddy, which was a cocktail that they both enjoyed. As far as I know, Victoria

Wade was a teetotaler and didn't join in. But these three women who lived on Joy Street were intelligent, they were hard working, and they were outstanding citizens of our community.

Just next door to the Wade Apartments was the office of The Montgomery Vindicator. This was our weekly newspaper, although there were two newspapers in the county then. The other was The Sevier County Republican, which was printed down on Main Street. In the past the Vindicator had been a very prominent weekly newspaper, not only in Sevier County, but all over East Tennessee. The editor and publisher was Captain Bill Montgomery, who founded the Vindicator and who was well know for his editorials and opinions in the newspaper. Captain Montgomery was known for his one-liners. That is, there would be a news story and maybe three or four paragraphs down in the story would be a couple lines of his opinions or ideas that had nothing to do with a news story but were thoughts that occurred to him while he was setting the type for the weekly press.

One of the strangest ones that I remember in the middle of a news story was this line, "The Sevier County Quarterly Court meets Monday. All Justices of the Peace who can read and write are urged to come in and subscribe to the Vindicator."

Captain Montgomery was also known to enjoy his toddy, perhaps at times to excess. During the time of Prohibition, he inserted in the middle of a story these lines, "The State of Kansas last week voted dry, but then who in the Hell wants to go to Kansas?"

When Captain Montgomery died, his son, Roy, became the editor and publisher. Roy was not the energetic newsman that his father was. As a matter of fact, it became something to watch the front page of the Vindicator as it was published (and Roy only published whenever he wanted to. It didn't come out every week.) But there were certain parts of the front page for which Roy never changed the type after his father died. There was one particular line that I found amusing and always looked for to see if it was still on the front page. This was a line down in a little box that said, "The bird of paradise has a wing span of six feet." I know this was on the front page of the Vindicator for more than a year, and as far as I know, was still there in the last issue.

Next door to the Vindicator, up on the corner of Joy Street and Park Road, lived Mrs. Thurman. Mrs. Thurman had the only angel food cake pan on the street and whoever made an angel food cake would have to go first to Mrs. Thurman and borrow her cake pan, and of course, make sure it was returned after the cake was baked. I remember my mother many times sending me up the street to borrow Mrs. Thurman's angel food cake pan. The baking of this cake occurred only when we had an excess of eggs, that is the hens had laid more eggs than we could otherwise eat for breakfast or for other purposes, and Mother would make an angel food cake.

Being the very conservative cook that she was, every time she made an angel food cake, which required a large number of egg whites, she also made a yellow cake which used the yellow yolks. Personally, I always liked yellow cake better than the angel food cake.

Pines Theater

JBW with Dolly Parton

DOCTORS, DRUG STORES, MILLS AND THEATRES

Sevierville had several medical doctors who I thought were very prominent people, highly respected men in the community, much more beloved and honored than I think doctors are today. I think the doctors in those days were good doctors, considering the times they practiced medicine in. They were smart men and had as good training and education as I suppose was available. And they were an interesting group in themselves.

Dr. R. A. Broady and his wife had been medical missionaries in China in the 1930s and came to Sevier County to practice in Sevierville before World War II got started. Mrs. Broady was a nurse and they were highly regarded for their concern and care.

Dr. C. P. Wilson had come to Sevierville as a State Health Department physician and stayed in Sevierville to practice. He finally opened Wilson's Hospital.

Dr. O. H. Yarberry was the one that I knew best because he lived right down the street from me. He lived on Court Avenue and his office was just half a block down in what is now the Ogle Building on the corner of Bruce Street and Court Avenue. Dr. Yarberry was a highly regarded physician and surgeon in the community and was an interesting man to watch because he was always in a hurry. Keep in mind this was the day of house calls. The doctors had their black bags, and when somebody got sick they called the doctor and the doctor got in his car and drove to the home to see the patient.

During that time Dr. Yarberry drove a Hudson Terraplane, which was probably one of the ugliest cars ever built. It was about as wide as it was long, and Dr. Yarberry always drove at breakneck speed. People literally cleared the roads for him, got out of his way for two reasons. One, they felt as if he was probably on an emergency call to somebody who was sick and needed his medical attention. And two, it was just safer to get out of the way of that Hudson Terraplane.

I used to walk the hundred or so feet down to the corner to watch Dr. Yarberry leave the house in the morning. Court Avenue then was a dead end at his house and he would pull in there. In the morning he would come out the front door of the house, get in his Hudson Terraplane and put it in reverse. He would then back all the way to his office at the corner of Bruce and Court Avenue, a little over a block. He had a black bird dog which always accompanied him and usually he would get going before the dog got to the car, so the dog would catch up about Joy Street and leap into the area between the hood and the right front fender, which was where he rode when Dr. Yarberry went on his house calls.

Later Dr. and Mrs. Yarberry and their son Horace moved to a home on Cedar Street across from the Methodist Church. Late one evening I went up there to see Horace. He was not at home, but Dr. Yarberry came driving up the street to the driveway. There was a ramp up from the street to the driveway and Dr. Yarberry would come up that ramp so fast he could almost get that Hudson Terroplane off the ground. As I said, he was always in a hurry. Mrs. Yarberry met him at the back door. She had been to her farm north of the river and had brought a pig home with her. The pig was in a crate near the back door.

"Dr. Yarberry," she said, "I want you to fix that pig's rupture."

I could tell that Dr. Yarberry did not want to operate on the pig, but Mrs. Yarberry had laid out his instruments on a table covered with old newspapers. She had a tomato can with cotton in the bottom and a can of ether. The ether can had a rubber nipple in the top and a safety pin was used to make a hole so the ether could be poured out of the can. Dr. Yarberry grabbed the pig by the hind legs and put him on the table.

"You give the anesthetic, Johnny," Dr. Yarberry said.

I poured the ether into the tomato can and put the pig's nose in the can. The pig went to sleep and Dr. Yarberry performed the needed surgery and quickly put the pig back on the crate.

Horace Yarberry later became a very prominent anesthesiologist at Baptist Hospital in Knoxville, but I think I gave an anesthetic before he did.

I loved both Dr. and Mrs. Yarberry. They were wonderful, interesting people.

Another prominent physician was Dr. R. A. McCall. Dr. McCall was considered one of the most brilliant physicians in the county. He had graduated from the University of Tennessee Medical School, and he had a reputation for staying up with the very latest developments in medicine. He did have a fault, as such. He would occasionally take a few days off and indulge to excess in the grape, but no one worried about that with Dr. McCall because every one would say, "Well, don't worry about it. If he's had to drink, he won't come and see you if you're sick." I remember Dr. Broady said that one reason Dr. McCall knew more about the latest trends in medicine than anybody else in the county was that Dr. McCall sobered up reading medical journals. Because of the frequency of these events, he always knew the latest medicine available.

At that time Sevierville had two drug stores. As a matter of fact, Sevierville had two of a lot of things, which we thought made us more than just a small town. We had two drug stores, two banks, two funeral homes, two hardware stores and you had a choice. We had more than two dry goods stores, and we felt as if we were a pretty good-sized small town. Anyway, we had two very interesting drug stores, both located on Court Avenue, just about a hundred or so feet apart..

Lee's Drug Store was owned by Dr. S. O. Lee. Up the street there was Williams Drug Store, owned by Dr. Williams. These two men were personalities indeed, but totally different types of people. Dr. Lee was a very kind, outgoing person who loved young people and his store was the hangout for young people. After school young people came to his soda counter and had ice cream and sodas and read his magazines, and Dr. Lee, who played the piano by ear, had a piano in the store and would play for the customers. Everybody had a good time and everybody loved Dr. Lee and he loved everybody.

Up the street was Dr. Williams. Dr. Williams was kind of a gruff old character and the older men frequented his drug store, standing around smoking their cigars and maybe occasionally drinking a Coca-Cola or something. Dr. Williams would give advice on medicine, perhaps more than he was supposed to.

It's amusing now, because then people called these druggists or pharmacists "Doctor". But Dr. Lee and Dr. Willliams were not doctors and occasionally they would try to make it clear that they were not to be called Doctor. The physicians didn't much like it that the pharmacists were called doctors, so they called them Mister. Today, I've noticed the pharmacists have a doctor's degree in pharmacy, but then today nobody calls them Doctor. So I suppose that's a sign of the change of times.

Anyway, these two drug stores we had in Sevierville then were pretty keen on competition. They competed for the community's business. Dr. Lee went out on some of the roads and put up billboards that said, "Lee has it. Lee's Drug Store, Sevierville, Tennessee. Lee has it." Right behind that Dr. Williams came up and put up a sign saying, "Williams sells it. Williams Drug Store, Sevierville, Tennessee. Williams sells it."

So people talked and laughed about these two advertisements. I suppose it did bring them both a lot of business. But they were both interesting men. Both played a large part in the character and personality of our city.

There were three mills in Sevierville that were very important to the economy of our town. Actually, out in the county there were a number of small grist mills or tub mills, as they were sometimes called. On small streams a raceway would be made upstream from the mill to get the water up over an overshot wheel, which would turn the mill, and there were still a number of those in the county when I was a small boy.

The mills in Sevierville, however, were pretty large. There was Temple Milling Company, which was owned by my wife Patsy's family, and had been at one time the Walker Milling Company. My father-in-law, Mr. John Temple, and his wife bought the mill when Walker went broke during the Depression. It was located on Bruce Street down about a block from my home. On down the street was Sevierville Grain and Feed Company, which had its mill on the river down at Catlettsburg, or what was then called Cobbtown, the name coming from the fact that the mill was there. A dam there ran the mill.

The Sevierville Mills, owned by the Wade family and later the Frost family, were located on Main Street in what we then called China Town. Why, I have no idea. There certainly never was a Chinaman down there. There was a dam across the East Prong of the Little Pigeon River to run this mill.

The Temple Mill was powered by a diesel engine which made a kind of thumping noise. You could always hear it when it started in the morning and were always aware of when they turned it off in the evening, even though you got used to it and you didn't hear it as it ran. But it rattled the windows in the Courthouse when it was going with a load on it.

The mills were interesting to me because they were so busy during harvest time. I remember seeing horse-drawn wagons as well as trucks backed up way past my house on Joy Street with loads of wheat or corn. At harvest time the farmers brought their wheat and corn in to the mill. The mill bought most of it and ground it into flour and cornmeal and sold it. The bran from it they made into various livestock feeds. A lot of the farmers, however, kept a portion of their grain on file in the mill. In other words, they kept it at the mill and the miller took a toll. The farmer would come in during the year and take out flour or cornmeal. He was given credit against the corn or wheat he had brought in at harvest time. That was an important part of farmers' diet and they saved a considerable amount of money by working that way. Later, when laws became more complex and the sales tax came into existence, the law prohibited what was then called "exchange."

At first Sevierville had the Park Theatre located where Bob Ogle's law office is now on Court Avenue, and it was a real delight for me as a young boy to go to the movies, especially on Saturday when there was always a Western. This was the day of Tom Mix or Ken Maynard and Tim McCoy and Buck Gibson. Later, of course, Gene Autry and others came along.

Dad converted what had been the J. B. Waters Motor Company at the corner of Court Avenue and Joy Street into Pines Theatre and I was just old enough to take a big interest in it. My mother and I basically ran the theatre because Dad was never too interested in the operation. She did all of the bookings of the movies and paid the bills, and was in general the manager. I opened and closed and saw that the popcorn was popped and the sweet shop opened up. I also learned to operate the projectors, at least as a relief operator.

One of the interesting things that we had at the Pines Theatre was country music shows. We had a stage and the theatre seated a little over seven hundred people. On Friday nights we would generally have a country music show. We would book shows from those country music performers who were available, mostly out of Knoxville. The "Midday Merry-Go-Round" was a popular WNOX program in Knoxville, headed up by Lowell Blanchard.

Lowell booked his country music stars out into schools and various locations for shows. They were always happy to come to the Pines Theatre because, for one reason, it was not far from Knoxville and it was easy to get to. Also, we had a good theatre and a good business and a good reputation for a country music show. Among the stars that came out there then was Archie Campbell, who had a act where he performed as "Grandpappy," as he called him. The Carlisle Brothers had a good country music act and a comedy act of "Hotshot Elmer" which went over well with the crowd. Other performers who later became bigger stars included Chet Atkins, who started out in Knoxville and played the Pines Theatre. Chet played with many entertainers in those days, including Bill Carlisle and the Carter Family. He toured with Red Foley, who also went on to the Grand Ole Opry.

The Carter Family, known as the First Family of Country Music, played the Pines Theatre many times. Mother Maybelle was a pioneer in country music and leader in this group. In addition, the original Carter Family featured her daughters, Anita, Helen and June. June was the comedy part of the act and later became better known as the wife of Johnny Cash. As far as I know, Johnny Cash never played the Pines Theatre. This was really before his day.

Bill and Charlie Monroe played the Pines Theatre several times and along with them was Lester Flatt, who became famous in his own right. Bill Monroe became extremely famous as father of bluegrass music.

Don Gibson, another well known performer out of the "Midday Merry-Go-Round" in Knoxville, was also a favorite at the Pines Theatre.

One of Knoxville's most famous acts was Homer and Jethro. Homer and Jethro had many hits, mostly in the comedy and novelty acts of their recordings. They could take a very popular song, even a pop song, and make it into a comedy hillbilly recording that sold a lot of records. Both of them were born in Knoxville. They came up on the "Midday Merry-Go-Round" and were at the Pines Theatre several times.

Peewee King was a favorite in country music in those days and was discovered by Gene Autrey. Pee Wee was really a Yankee, but he migrated into Kentucky, where he had a radio show, and later even went to Hollywood. But he was at the "Midday Merry-Go-Round" in Knoxville on WNOX for a time and he played the Pines Theatre even later, after he left the "Midday Merry-Go-Round."

The Louvin Brothers, Ira and Charlie, did a kind of act that was really popular with a mandolin and a guitar and great country voices.

The little town of Maynardville, Tennessee, was the birthplace of a number of well-known country artists, including Roy Acuff. Roy, even in the times of the Pines Theatre, was a star of the Grand Ole Opry. He did, however, one time play the Pines Theatre. He was scheduled to come into Sevierville with a big tent. They put the tent up in a bottom just outside of town. That day there was a terrible rain storm and it was so muddy that nobody could get to the tent. Dad went out and got hold of Roy and suggested he move the act to the Pines Theatre, which he did. It was a very successful show and Roy came back one other time. Roy's act was well known in Sevier County because Cousin Oswald Kirby was a local Sevier County native born up in Walden's Creek.

Also from the Maynardville area was Chet Atkins. Another star, also a great country music performer, was Carl Smith. He came out of Maynardville also and was in Knoxville on Radio Station WROL, which was a little bit of competition for WNOX. WROL had some great music shows and the morning show on WROL was the big "Cas Walker Show". Cas started an awful lot of country music entertainers on their way. Cas's performers also played the Pines Theatre many times and it was not unusual at all for Cas to come out and emcee an act. Cas started a procedure of having an amateur hour where he would let local people come in and play.

A "Cas Walker Amateur Hour" was the first time Dolly Parton ever played the Pines Theatre. Dolly was just a small girl, maybe six years old. I remember that night. The guitar was bigger than Dolly. But even then she was a fantastically great performer. I've always bragged a little bit about Dolly and the Pines Theatre because I think that was the first time Dolly ever played to a paid audience. She had obviously sung in a lot of churches and community groups, but this time it was a paying audience. Sevier County is indeed proud of Dolly. She has truly been a great asset to our community.

Smilin' Eddy Hill was another Knoxville performer who came to our theater on later occasions and went on to Nashville and became a radio performer and disc jockey. Eddy Hill was a great musician and, if I remember correctly, he brought drums to the Pines Theatre for a show one night, the first time that I ever remember drums brought into a country music show. You wouldn't think of country music today without drums, but back in those days he broke the ice on drums in country music.

Among the more regional stars who played the Pines Theatre were Bonnie Lou and Buster. There were a number of others that I wish I had kept better records on, because the show ran most every Friday night for a number of years through the latter part of the forties and into the fifties.

Occasionally we would get a show that wasn't out of Nashville or Knoxville. I well remember when Tex Ritter played the Pines Theatre and we got acquainted with Tex. Tex and I became friends later on. He was a great star and played the Pines Theatre at least two or three times. Lash Larue played the Pines. His whip act was very popular with the crowd.

Television in the mid-fifties closed down the small town and neighborhood theaters and Pines Theatre fell along with the rest of them, but it was a great time for entertainment during those years. Pines Theatre generally tried to have a class A show on Monday and Tuesday, and then on Wednesday and Thursday have maybe a double feature with what we called an "action picture." Then on Friday we had another action picture followed by the country music show, and then run the film a second time. On Saturday it was always a cowboy western. Charles Starrett, the Three Musketeers, Bob Steel, Ken Maynard and Tex Ritter were the main stars of the Pines Theatre Saturday shows.

During that time, across the street in the Dwight Wade house lived Dwight and his wife, Kate, and their oldest son, Dwight Wade, Jr., who for many years now has been a prominent internal medicine physician in Knoxville. But during that time Dwight was another young lad who lived in the town, asked a lot of questions and was curious about everything. It was not unusual for a young lad to sit in the movies and look back at where the light came out of the projection machine and wonder how all that happened with the projection machine and how the light got on the screen. Most didn't have the nerve to climb up the steps in the dark to come up where the projection booth was, but one Saturday I was up there in the projection booth running a Tex Ritter movie. I looked up at the door and there stood Dwight, Jr., probably about six or seven years old.

And Dwight, Jr. says, "Is old Tex in there?"

"Yeah," I said, "he's in this movie, Dwight, Jr."

He looked funny and says, "Tell him Dwight, Jr. says, 'Hi.'" Then he turned around and left. I enjoyed running the projections there and working in the Pines Theatre. A lot of people got pleasure from the movies in those times in Sevierville.

JOBS

When I was twelve years old I got a job carrying The Knoxville News-Sentinel. The job of a paper boy back then was considered a real plum for any kid who wanted to work and earn a few extra bucks. The Sentinel at that time was an evening newspaper and it cost twenty-five cents a week to get the paper six days a week plus Sunday. If you didn't want the Sunday paper you could get the rest of the week for fifteen cents.

I got the job carrying the Sentinel and I worked pretty hard at building up my route. Pretty soon I had the biggest route in town. I had two young lads working for me, carrying the paper in certain sections of the town that I didn't want to get to on the main route. I had about one hundred and fifty customers and I made about fifteen dollars a week.

There was a lot to learn carrying the paper. You had to sell. You sold to get your subscribers. Obviously you had delivery tasks. You had to deliver the paper satisfactorily to them, trying to get it in dry and keeping the customers happy by getting the paper where they wanted it.

Then you had to collect. I usually collected on Friday, then on Saturday the paper man came from Knoxville and I paid my bill. You had to collect enough money to pay your bill. A lot of paper boys made the mistake of collecting only enough money to pay their bill, then they would go to Lee's Drug Store and sit around the counter eating ice cream or sandwiches until the paper man got there, paid their bill and left. If you did that you never made any profit because your profit came last. But it was an interesting job and good training for a young entrepreneur who was just starting out in the cold, bitter world of business. I enjoyed the job very much and learned a lot about people carrying The Knoxville News-Sentinel.

A newspaper boy has contact with many households, and its not surprising that you learn that the people who have a reputation for wealth and position are sometimes a little more difficult to deal with. I had one experience with a very wealthy, prominent man in town, highly regarded in the community in terms of his position, was one of my customers. But I simply couldn't collect from the guy. I had to find him, and I couldn't get into his office and I couldn't find him at home or anywhere except maybe on the street somewhere, and it was just very difficult to collect from him. So I quit him. I just decided I wouldn't carry his paper.

Well, he got very upset and called my dad and said, "You know, Johnny's not delivering my paper any more."

So Dad called me in and said, "Hey, what's the trouble here? You know, you're not delivering this man's paper, and he's a very influential man. What's the problem?"

I said, "Well, the problem is I can't collect from him. I can't ever find him to get my money. I can't get in his office, I can't collect at home from his wife, and I have to be paid for this paper every week. I have to pay my bill and I'm not going to carry his paper unless he pays me."

Well, I think it kind of tickled Dad a little bit because I think he was glad to go back and tell this leader what the story was. But after that arrangements were made so that every Friday when I delivered his paper, his secretary handed me twenty-five cents. So we got along pretty well.

Almost the opposite of that experience, there was a woman on my route who lived alone and whose general reputation was not good from the standpoint of character. I was told, "Boy, you know, you'd beterer watch her. She'll beat you out of the paper. You won'd be able to collect from her." But I found the truth to be the opposite. Every Saturday when I went to collect there was twenty-five cents under the mat at the front door. It never failed; it was always there. So I learned you'd better be careful about what people say about somebody. You may have a little different experience.

Another man was considered to be a little bit outside the law. He was kind of a wheeler-dealer kind of a man that some people said might be a little crooked. But I had a good experience with this man too. As a matter of fact, he was the only person on my route of 150 who consistently gave me a good tip. This was my first experience with tips, and I learned that if you have an opportunity to give good service to some people, it generally will pay off. This man would ask me a couple of things about where I put the paper and one thing and another, and I tried to comply with that and found it to be worthwhile, especially with him, because he gave me a good tip.

I carried the paper and did real well with it. I never shall forget the time came when I had saved a hundred. I had one hundred one-dollar bills hidden in a secure hidey place in my bedroom. Well, as a young lad of that age, I actually thought that was probably all the money I was ever going to need, and it was really nice to have that. Finally, I said something to Mother or Dad about it and they encouraged me to put it in the bank, and I did. But at that point in time a hundred dollars was some money and I was very proud to have it.

I decided it was time to quit the route. It was time to do some other things, so I told Mother and Dad, "Well, I'm going to quit my route."

They said, "Well, that's your business, whatever you want to do. Have you decided what you're going to do with it, who you're going to give it to? What's going to happen to the route?"

I said, "Yeah, I have. I've thought a lot about that. I'd going to give my route to Mr. C   ." I won't give the man's full name because he still has a lot of relatives in this town and they're all very fine people.

Dad said, "You're going to give it to Mr. C   ? How did you come to that conclusion?"

I said, "Well, I know Mr. C   has a large family and they're very poor. They're about the poorest people in town. The kids don't have clothes and I don't think they have enough to eat all the time and Mr. C works for the city. He's a street sweeper for the City of Sevierville and I found out he just makes twelve dollars a week. He can take this route and he can make fifteen dollars a week and he might make more if he works at it hard enough."

Well, I saw immediately that this surprised my father, and he took me out on the front porch and he sat me down in one of those green wicker chairs and said, "Son, I'm really very proud that you would think about Mr. C   and his problems. You're absolutely right. They are very poor people, but he can't handle your route."

I said, "Why not?"

He said, "Son, Mr. C is illiterate. He can't read or write. There's no way that he could keep track of his accounts and collect."

Well, talk about a first early lesson in the value of education. That one hit me very solidly and I resolved to be a little bit better student. I had an appreciation for education that I don't think I ever forgot from that day.

The summer of my fifteenth year (actually, I became sixteen on July 15th in that summer) was a good summer for me. World War II had just ended, but we were far from being back to normal. A lot of items were still rationed in the community and there was a shortage of a lot of other items. They hadn't built a new car for sale to the public since 1941. The '40's were the last cars sold to the public. In the fall of 1946, the first post-war new cars came out for public sale.

There was a shortage of tires and shoes and sugar and a lot of things, but we began to try to get back to some normal life in 1946. After I got out of school that spring, I knew I needed a pretty good job, so I went down to Stokely's Canning Factory because that's where a lot of people went to get a job. Stokely's paid forty cents an hour and that was considered really good wages.

Mr. Buckner was the manager and I knew Mr. Buckner. As a matter of fact, he lived down on Court Avenue. I knew his family real well. So I went down there and asked for a job. They put me to stacking pea vines. When the peas were mowed and harvested, they brought them in to Stokely Canning Factory in Sevierville and they took the peas off to go through a sheller and into cans. But the vines came out of a pea viner. The job involved a pitchfork to haul these vines back and you made a huge stack. I've seen some stacks of pea vines that would be maybe twenty by thirty or forty, and maybe ten feet high or more. Those vines sat in the stacks and kind of cured, and then they were used to feed cattle. But hauling those vines back — let me tell you what. After about an hour you were green from your feet to the top of your head. So I did that for a week and I decided that I wanted a little bit better job than stacking pea vines, even for the summer.

So I told Mother and Dad I wanted to go up to Gatlinburg and see if I could get a job at the Hotel Greystone. My sister, Mary Louise had worked there one summer when she was in college as a secretary in the office, and the owner of the Greystone, Mr. Dick Whaley, and his wife Martha were friends of the family. So I decided that I'd go to Mr. Whaley for a job and

Dad and Mother okayed it.

I went up to Mr. Whaley and told him I'd like to have a job for that summer. He said, "Yeah, have you got a driver's license?"

Well, I did. I had a driver's license even though I was just fifteen years old. He said, "You're going to drive the hotel car here, which means that you're going to meet each of the six buses that come into Gatlinburg each day. A lot of times there will be people on those buses that are be our guests at the Greystone. You bring those people and their bags all here."

This service had been started during the war because of the gas rationing and shortage of other transportation.

"Also," he said, "you're going to be the assistant bellhop." He had another full-time bellhop who had been there for a long time. I was his assistant, and I was to go to work at ten o'clock in the morning and work until ten o'clock at night, and after six o'clock the regular bellhop went off duty and I had the whole job of bellhop from six o'clock on. However, most of the people checked in before six o'clock, so I would have only three or four more people checking in after six. But anyway, I made fifteen dollars a week, but I got tips, and I learned to cultivate these tips.

When it was time for a bus to come in, generally from Knoxville, I would get in the car and drive to the bus station and sit around until the bus got there. The Gatlinburg Inn had a car at the bus station, as well as the Riverside Hotel and the Mountain View.

There was a friendly competition among us. If some driver didn't make the bus that particular hour and there were passengers for his hotel, one of the other hotel drivers without passengers would take the passengers to the proper hotel. So I got to know the drivers and it was really very interesting work.

One of the most interesting people I met was Wesley Jake Reagan, called Jake. He was the driver for the Mountain View, and Jake was one of the most loyal employees I ever met. He thought that there was absolutely no place equal or even close to being equal to the Mountain View Hotel. He loved the Mountain View, and he thought that Mr. Andy Huff, the owner of the Mountain View, was without a doubt the best man in Gatlinburg and the best man that Wesley Reagan knew. And, you know, the truth is, that Wesley was pretty much right about Mr. Huff. He was a highly regarded and respected man in Gatlinburg.

Wesley drove a 1940 black, four-door Packard convertible, a beautiful automobile. I was very envious of Jake's car. I was driving a '41 Oldsmobile. Jake kept his car in perfect, tiptop, clean shape and when he came through town with the top down, it was really a sight to see. Of course, we liked to kid each other, and when we found out something about each other, we weren't above playing a little bit of a joke on each other, sometimes more than a little bit of a joke. At any rate, one day I was in the Greystone and they said, "Mr. Whaley wants to see everybody in his office."

So I went back in the office and Dick Whaley said, "We're going to have a very important guest at the Greystone. Mr. and Mrs. Andy Huff are going to come to the Greystone. The reason for this is that Mr. Huff had an allergy that's giving him a lot of trouble, and some of the doctors have decided that those trees around the Mountain View may be contributing to his allergy, and during this coming month they'd like him to get away from those trees and see if this helps him any. So Mr. and Mrs. Huff are going to move into the Greystone for a month.

"And," he added, "obviously, we want Mr. and Mrs. Huff treated with every courtesy."

So I thought, "Boy, that's really something, Mr. Huff's coming over to the Greystone." So I went to meet the bus that afternoon and we were sitting on the steps going up to the bus station. The drivers from the Riverside and the Gatlinburg Inn were there, and here comes Jake. I turned to one of the drivers and said, "Have you heard that things are getting pretty bad over at the Mountain View?"

He said, "No, I hadn't."

Well, Jake popped up and said, "They ain't nothing wrong with the Mountain View, I'll tell you that. You're wrong about that."

I said, "Well, you know, maybe I am, but I hear things are pretty bad over there, so bad that, as a matter of fact, Mr. and Mrs. Huff are going to move out of the Mountain View."

Oh, my goodness, Jake just jumped up and said, "That's a lie and that's not true and whoever told you that doesn't know what they're talking about. That's ridiculous and simply not true."

Well, we got a pretty good rise out of that. I happened to know the desk clerk over at the Mountain View at that time. I made arrangements with him so that when the Huffs were ready to check out, I drove up in the Greystone car at the front door of the Mountain View. Here came Mr. and Mrs. Huff and I put their bags in the Greystone car and took them to the Greystone. And Jake was standing there at the front of his Packard absolutely speechless. He couldn't believe what he was seeing.

Anyway, they came over to the Greystone and stayed there for about a month and everybody was honored to have them. Came time for Mr. Huff to leave and he walked up to the desk clerk, a fellow called Tubby. Mr. Huff asked for his bill and Tubby said, "Mr. Huff, there is no bill. You're here compliments of Mr. Whaley."

Well, this was back in the day when a lot of that kind of thing went on. Mr. Huff said, "I want my bill and I intend to pay for this."

Well, the sweat just popped out on Tubby's head (he was a little bit overweight anyway), and he said, "But, Mr. Huff, if I take your money, Mr. Whaley will fire me."

Well, Mr. Huff stood there for a little bit, then said, "Well, I understand what you're saying. I'll have to find another way to settle this debt." And so he left.

Talking about Tubby, he was kind of a little bit of a grouch and he would fuss at people and boss the help around. He was always kind of bossing me around. I always called him Mister, and gave him a lot of respect.

But as I said, I came to work at ten o'clock in the morning. I was entitled to my meals, but that was kind of an awkward time. Breakfast was over and they were getting ready for lunch. Mrs. Parton was one of the head cooks back in the kitchen, so I'd always go back there and say, "Mrs. Parton, is there anything I can do for you this morning?" And lots of times she'd have some little job like getting some little thing that was heavy for her out of the freezer or cooler, or carry out some garbage, or do some little something.

And always, when I got done doing whatever she wanted me to do, she'd say, "Now, Johnny, you sit down over there and I'll fix you breakfast." So I'd sit down at the table there where the help was and she'd fix my breakfast. Man, I tell you, I had a good breakfast! I had hot biscuits, eggs, country ham. She fed me pretty good.

I'm sitting there eating one morning and in comes Tubby. He sees me sitting there eating all this breakfast and he just has a fit. He says, "What do you mean, being in here? The help's not supposed to be back in here interfering with the kitchen. If you were going to eat breakfast in here, you were supposed to be here at breakfast time. I want you out of this kitchen and I don't ever want to see you in here eating any more."

Well, that was about all that got said, because about that time Mrs. Parton grabbed him. I can't repeat all the things she said, but she said, "You big, fat slob, you get out of my kitchen. You stay away from this kitchen. This boy's the only one around here that helps me do anything, and if I want to fix his breakfast, I'm going to fix his breakfast and you don't have a thing to say about what's going on back here and I don't want you back here. Get out!"

Well, that was kind of an event!

That afternoon I was standing at the front door of the Greystone where I would stand when I didn't have anything to do, and open the door for guests coming in and out, and here comes Mr. Whaley. He'd been off on some other business out of the hotel and I hadn't seen him that day, but I opened the door for him and said, "Good afternoon, Mr. Whaley."

He says, "Hi, Johnny. Did you enjoy your breakfast this morning?" There wasn't much that went on around the Hotel Greystone that Dick Whaley didn't know. He was one of the finest men I ever knew and I learned a lot from him in how to deal with people and how to manage people. He treated everybody in a fair and courteous way, but there was something about his demeanor that told you that he expected a high performance.

Working for tips is a good experience and one that I think is good for any young person to have. Gatlinburg was a good place for that. A lot of girls and boys waited on tables in the hotels and restaurants and got tips. Being a bellhop was an experience for me that I enjoyed doing — checking people in and doing little services for them, and you got a little tip, a twenty-five cent tip. Back then that was pretty good.

But as I have mentioned, after six o'clock I was in charge as the bellhop. So I had learned to go to the register and see what reservations we had left that day, people who had not checked in but were due to check in on that particular day. There would be a few, three or four at the most. I would see what these people's names were and where they were from, anything about them. Since World War II had just ended, it wasn't unusual for us to have a veteran or even somebody still in uniform. We also had a lot of honeymooners, people coming back from the war and getting married and coming up to Gatlinburg for their honeymoon and staying at the Hotel Greystone, which was quite a treat.

So I would learn what I could about those people, then wait for them on the porch and lots of times when a car drove in I was able to know who it was. I remember specifically that one time I noticed on the reservation list that Captain and Mrs. Parker from Alabama had reservations at the Greystone for the day and they hadn't checked in. So I was standing on the porch when this car with Alabama plates on it drove up to the front and inside were this young man and woman, and it was pretty easy to see they were just married. The new brides nearly always had a corsage on their dress, and sure enough Mrs. Parker had on her corsage, even though the captain was not in uniform.

I went down and opened the door and said, "Captain and Mrs. Parker, welcome to the Greystone. Mr. Dick Whaley, the owner of the Greystone, has asked me to make sure that you're properly taken care of, so I'll be glad to check you in."

So I got them in to the desk, checked them in and took their bags on to their room. I had learned early that there was nothing that makes people feel good like using their name. It generated a good tip, and I recall Captain Parker indeed gave me a nice tip for my efforts that night.

If I really wanted to go a little further than usual for a tip, and I knew somebody was going to check in, I'd go up to their room, take the towels all out, put them back in the linen closet on that floor, and when I checked them in I'd say, "Oh, the maids have not left you clean towels. I'll be right back." So I'd go back, get the towels back out and put them in the room. I guess a lot of people weren't used to service in World War II and this always generated a good tip.

So I learned to work for tips and I learned to like people, and I learned a valuable lesson — that the finest people, the biggest people, were the easiest ones to please and the ones that appreciated more than anybody else courtesy and service. Working at the Greystone was a great experience.

Fortunately for me, twenty years later I joined together with a group of men and bought the Hotel Greystone.

The Sevier County Courthouse

LIFE IN SEVIERVILLE: THE COURTHOUSE

At the time I grew up in Sevierville, the Sevier County Courthouse was the center not only for Sevierville but for all of Sevier County. News of happenings in the remote sections of the county generally came to the courthouse and it was there that people came, especially on Saturday.

During those years I don't think there was a single office in the courthouse that had more than one room, a vault and a small storage room, with which to perform its functions. The Register of Deeds was in a very small office with a vault. The County Court Clerk had a rather large single room, as did the Clerk and Master, the Trustee, and the Superintendent of Roads. These, along with the Tax Assessor's equally small office, were all on the first floor. On the second floor, the Circuit Court Clerk and the Superintendent of Schools each had one-room offices. There were two courtrooms, one upstairs and one down.

As I got a little older and got a little more nerve to run around, I soon learned the names of the office holders and the employees in the courthouse. One of my favorite people in the courthouse was Haskell Ogle, the Circuit Court Clerk. He served in that capacity for twenty-four years.

During those years, one of the things that Jimmie Temple and I would do was to look for Oliver DeLozier in the afternoons. He carried the Knoxville News-Sentinel, which was then an afternoon paper. (The Knoxville Journal was the morning paper.) Oliver had a large route and carried the papers on his bicycle. In later years Oliver became an outstanding OB-Gyn physician and delivered both of my children. But in those years he was the paper boy.

Jimmie and I would watch for Oliver on his route through town and ask him if he had any extra papers. Sometimes the newspaper would send him more papers than he had customers. Many times he would give us an extra copy and we would take it to Haskell Ogle on the second floor of the courthouse and see if he would buy it. He always agreed to the purchase and gave us a nickel. If we didn't have a paper, we'd still go up to Haskell's office and he would give us a nickel to fight. We'd put on a little bit of a fighting show and he'd generally give us a nickel anyway.

When we got the nickel we'd go to one of the drugstores where we could buy two cones of ice cream. Jimmie was always envious of me because I could eat the ice cream much slower than he could. I would lick it very carefully and take some time to eat it, whereas Jimmie kind of gobbled his down, biting off hunks of the ice cream, sometimes eating it so fast the cold of the ice cream would go to his head and give him a terrible headache.

We looked forward to our visits to Haskell Ogle. He was a very good friend to all the children in the town.

During part of my youth the county judge, then called Chairman of the Quarterly County Court, was Mr. Conley Huskey from Pittman Center. Conley was always interested in politics and was a close friend to Haskell Ogle. At one time they were roomers in our house at 107 Joy Street. I would pick up a little extra money by running chores for them, such as bringing wood up for the fire in the grate in the bedroom that was rented. Mr. Huskey was a very prominent citizen. He became the first Mayor of Pittman Center and accumulated a lot of land in the Pittman Center area.

The sheriffs were always interesting people in Sevier County. The jail, what we called the "old jail," was just behind the courthouse. I don't remember what year they finally tore it down, maybe in the early 1950s or late '40s. They built another jail right in the same place. As kids we didn't go around the jail too much. We would go down and stand on the outside and watch them bring in people who had been arrested, but we were a little afraid to go in too much. Occasionally, we might go in the door if the sheriff or a deputy would allow us to come in and loaf around a little bit. But we were always a bit afraid of the jail.

At one time Jimmie Temple's relative, Roy Fox, was Sheriff of Sevier County. Later Roy Whaley was sheriff for many years. At that time the sheriff ran for two-year terms and the law allowed him to serve three terms, so a sheriff could serve for six years. After Whaley, Fred Pierce and then Ray Noland served in that office. Some time after Ray a very colorful man named Bat Gibson was the sheriff.

It was always interesting to know what was going on in the jail. Sevier County didn't have much criminal activity then. There might be one shooting of some sort a year and maybe even one murder, and a few break-ins and stealing of chickens or pigs and that sort of thing. But generally Sevier County was a law-abiding county. People protected their own land and looked after their property, and there wasn't much crime. Of course, there were always the moonshiners. People up in the mountainous areas, particularly toward Cocke County, made white liquor and the sheriffs always made a big to-do about raiding the stills, bringing in the stills and liquor and beating up the stills. They generally did this right before election. After election it was a long time before they captured another still.

When summertime came, the Sevier County Courthouse, and especially the yard outside the courthouse, was used for a new and interesting purpose. People came to the courthouse, set up stands and sold whatever product they had for sale. The most common were patent medicine purveyors.

They usually had a truck that they could open from either the side or the back and make into a very small stage. They would have some kind of entertainment to attract the crowd, maybe some music, a magic show, sometimes an animal like a monkey on a leash, anything to attract attention and gather a crowd. But their main purpose was to sell their patent medicine, which was usually a tonic in a half-pint bottle guaranteed to cure a whole list of ailments and diseases. As a matter of fact, the claims made for these various medicines were unbelievable. They would heal absolutely anything, according to the purveyors. They were usually made of a mixture of herbs in an alcoholic solution. My dad told me the medicines were a type of beverage alcohol, and a lot of the benefit was to get the buzz from drinking the alcohol, especially those people who, for religious or other purposes, didn't want to drink whiskey or liquor, but were willing to take a tonic as medicine.

A number of these patent medicine guys came to Sevierville, but one came several times that I remember. He billed himself as Dr. Mockyton. He had a pretty good show and was a real carnival-like sales person. He made all kinds of claims about his medication. He claimed that he got his tonic from an old Indian recipe that a chief had given to his family. Dr. Mockyton claimed that he had been very sick, this tonic had cured him and he then recognized how important it was in the treatment of any number of diseases and complaints. I particularly remember him stating that he had been fatally ill on five occasions, at which times this medicine saved his life.

I talked to my mother about that and she said that truly the medication must be very potent because, if he'd been fatally ill five times, that meant that he had died five times and the medicine had brought him back to life. I don't think even Dr. Mockyton was really trying to claim that; but, he did say that his elixir would prolong life.

One of the techniques he used was to get a person from the crowd to come up and he would ask them if they had any kind of complaint, aches or pains. He knew how to pick these people and generally he knew how to find someone who had some type of complaint. He would tell them he was going to demonstrate how powerful his tonic was by rubbing a few drops on the back of their neck and ask them if they could taste this medication. I'm not sure what was in the medication, but most would respond by saying they could taste it. Then he would ask them if they felt better, and they would always say that they did, that they felt much better, and he would give them a bottle of his tonic. Then he commenced to sell the rest for a dollar a bottle. It was amazing to see how much Dr. Mockyton would sell with this sales approach.

Patent medicine salesmen were not the only people in the courthouse yard. There were also drummers who would set up stands. I remember people selling all sorts of gadgets or tools that they liked to demonstrate. Knife sharpeners and knives were popular items, and I remember some sales of blankets, especially Indian blankets that supposedly came from the West.

Occasionally, we would have performers who came in and got various merchants to sponsor their shows, during which they would advertise the merchants' products. One I remember was a middle-aged guy billing himself as the "Human Fly." He was a pretty pitiful spectacle. He had a costume obviously made out of a pair of long-handled underwear. On the back was painted what looked like fly wings, and there was some other ornamentation as well. The man was a little bit overweight. He advertised that he was going to climb the outside of the courthouse. The courthouse was four stories high with a steeple on top, so he had a pretty good crowd there to watch him. He had obviously done some climbing in the past, although I think this "human fly" was past his prime climbing age. But he got up pretty high and he would wave off and make little speeches about being sponsored by Cash Hardware Company and Frigidaire refrigerators and stoves.

There was an old man named Mr. Romines standing there in a pair of overalls and a felt hat. This Mr. Romines was at least in his late seventies, probably even into his eighties, and somebody that knew him said, "Why, Romines, you can climb better than that man can." And sure enough, Mr. Romines walked up to the corner of the building and climbed up into the third floor area.

There was big applause and a lot of cat calls and yells, and it had a dampening effect on the Human Fly's performance in Sevierville on that day.

Another patent medicine salesman that I remember coming occasionally to Sevierville billed himself as Black Bart. He had been sent to the penitentiary for some crime earlier in his life, and he attracted attention with some terrible-looking leg irons and chains that he had supposedly worn while working on a Georgia chain gang. He sold a patent medicine, but he was also a sort of preacher. So he told about how bad he had been and how he had repented and became somewhat of a preacher, but then he had this patent medicine that he claimed, along with religion, was what you really needed in your life. He did a pretty good job of it.

Of course, preachers, especially these roving evangelists, were at the courthouse pretty frequently. They were what people in those times called "Hellfire and brimstone" preachers, and what someone labeled as "Suckback" preachers. That was identified to me as a preacher who talked so loud and so long that he failed to stop to get his breath until he absolutely had to. Then, when he did run out of breath., there was this huge sucking noise where he sucked his breath back into his lungs so he could go on.

These preachers weren't too much of a problem until later, when public address systems and sound-powered systems came into play and they got so loud on the courthouse that officials finally had to stop them.

DINNER IS AT NOON

As I look back, life in Sevierville during the days of my childhood was pretty well structured. There was a routine which, in general, everybody followed, whatever their station in the community might be. For example, dinner (the big meal) then was at noon and there was very little eating in restaurants. Everyone in the town literally went home for dinner. The food on the table was about the same at every house. I don't mean to imply that there weren't some who lived on a level better than others. But the food was very, very similar everywhere.

It was not as bad as the way my father told things were when he was growing up as a young boy over in Blount County. He told that during those times their station in life was determined by what they used to sweeten their food. The very wealthy used granulated sugar, white sugar. The less well-to-do used honey, and at the bottom of the list, the poorest used molasses. I don't think that was true in Sevierville in my early days. Everyone pretty much had sugar to use for sweetening. But the menu on the table would have been similar in every house.

The acquiring, preservation and cooking of food was considerably different in those days from today's practices. Milk was an important part of the diet in Sevierville and most families had a cow. In the general neighborhoods in Sevierville there was a small barn behind the dwelling house. There were large pasture fields at the edge of town. One to the west of town was the Thomas farm, which later became the home of my uncle, E. W. "Cap" Paine. There was a field to the south just beyond the Murphy College site, which later became the Church of God Home for Children. I'm sure there was one to the east as well, but I don't really remember.

The family cows were taken to these pastures early in the mornings by a ranger. These were young boys who picked up some extra money by doing this job. W. T. (Bill) Atchley was one of the rangers I remember. In the evening, along about five, the ranger would go the field and get the cows, maybe twenty or thirty of them, and drive them into the town and up and down the streets. It was always surprising that every cow knew which driveway to turn into to go to her own barn.

Most times the mother of the family would come out and milk, feed and water the cow, which stayed in the barn until morning when the mother again milked the cow and gave it a small portion of grain or crushed cow feed. When the ranger came along, the cow walked out to the driveway and the ranger took the cows back to the pasture field for that day and the cycle was then repeated.

I well remember as a small child hearing the cow bells as the cows walked to and from the pasture field and hearing the lowing of the cows in the herd.

Almost every family also had a chicken lot to the rear of their home, where they kept hens for eggs that were gathered daily. Eggs were another important part of the diet. Also, it was not unusual for the family to raise fryers, young chickens raised up to about two pounds. These fryers were then killed for meat that was generally served to the family on Sunday. Sometimes a hen would be baked or stewed, but the smaller, younger chickens were fried. This was a different kind of fried chicken than you see in the fast food stores of today. The pieces were washed and dusted lightly with flour and seasonings, then fried in lard in an iron skillet, sometimes followed by a small amount of water and a lid for a quick steaming. The result was admittedly somewhat greasy when compared to today's fried chicken, but much more tasty than what people today know as fried chicken.

My father generally bought twenty or so capons each year, a capon being a rooster castrated when it was very young. These capons were fattened and were really and truly a delicacy, some of the finest meals I can recall. When we were to have capon for dinner, my father, my brother or I would go out into the chicken lot with a long, six-foot wire that had a U hook on the end of it. You got close to the bird and reached down and caught him by his foot. You then tied the feet together and took the chicken and laid him in the grass right near the back door of the house. Mother came out the back of the house through a screen door on the porch and onto a short walk. The walk took a turn toward the smokehouse and wash house where the family wash was done.

My mother always moved in a fast manner. I never saw her move slowly, never in my life, and I can still see her coming out the back door. About the time the screen door slammed closed, mother would turn that corner at the sidewalk, reach down and pick up that chicken by the neck, and with one swing around, the head came off and the chicken flopped in the grass. Mother went on to the smokehouse, picked up whatever she had come for, went back into the house to get the kettle, which had been placed on the stove to boil water, and came back to the yard with the scalding water to loosen the feathers and dress the chicken for cooking.

This was before the days of the supermarkets of today, although there were a number of small grocery stores or meat markets in the town. As you went down Court Avenue from our home on Joy Street there was the B & Y (Blazer and Yarberry) Market. On down the street was the Park Food Market, which the Newman family owned and operated for many, many years (later becoming Newman's Supermarket). And on down on the left was a small White Store, which later became a very fine family-owned chain of supermarkets. On up Bruce Street was John Emert's Market, a meat market, and up on Park Road were Arlie McCown's Meat Market, Mr. Seaton's Grocery Store, and Joe Hill's Grocery Store. I'm probably leaving some out. There were a number of markets and some came and went depending on the relative success of their operation.

All these markets had delivery boys who delivered on bicycles. My mother would call the market on the telephone. She would ask what they had in terms of fresh vegetables ... beans or potatoes or whatever she wanted ... and she would always ask the quality and price of those items. She would place her order and then the delivery boy would bring the groceries to the house and receive his pay. I well remember that my mother did not hesitate to send items back to the store if the quality was not up to her standards.

Later on Fred Atchley and his wife, Elizabeth, opened what I suppose should be considered the first supermarket in Sevierville. It was a larger market down on the public square and this consolidated some of the smaller markets. Mr. Atchley also operated what were known as Atchley's Rolling Stores. These were large trucks that looked a whole lot like today's school buses. They were stocked with groceries and other items such as cleaning materials that the housewife might need. Usually on top was a coop of chickens to be sold or traded. These rolling stores went into the country on regular routes, stopping at houses so that housewives could come out and buy, sell or barter. Eggs and chickens were frequently swapped for flour and meal and other grocery items. A lot of trading went on. Rolling stores were important in those days before World War II.

I mentioned that many families had milk cows, but there were dairies as well. As a matter of fact, my father operated the Sunnyside Dairy Farm in Love Addition. He had a relatively small dairy operation, about thirty cows and a horse-drawn wagon that generally was driven by a man named Ashley Sutton. Mr. Sutton and his family milked the cows, bottled the milk and delivered milk in the town. So my family never had a cow at home because we had the dairy. The Yett family operated a much larger dairy. They were the first to pasteurize milk.

Milk then was in bottles, delivered by the milk man and left on the door step. It was whole milk. You could see the rich cream at the top of the bottle and below that the milk. The housewife generally took the cream off for use in cooking or coffee or mixed it into the whole milk, depending on how the family liked to drink their milk. If she took the cream off the top, the bottom was a much thinner drink without the milk fat and was referred to as Bluejohn. I recall having a dislike for Bluejohn, much preferring the whole milk.

Ice was an interesting commodity that was very important to the housewife for the preservation of foods and beverages. The ice house was situated next to Sevierville Mills, near where Carl Ownby's Hardware Company is today, on the left bank of the East Prong of the Little Pigeon River. The ice wagon was pulled by a team of Clydesdale horses like those seen pulling the Budweiser wagons today. The ice man loaded up his ice from the ice house and had his tongs, which looked like huge steel pliers, to pick up ice. He drove around the town. Each housewife had cards with numbers on each side. One side read "25," another "50," another "75" and the final side said "100." These were the pounds of your order. If you wanted 50 pounds of ice you put your card in your window with the "50" up. The ice man saw the card, stopped, took his ice pick and cut off from the large hunk what he estimated to be fifty pounds of ice. He then got his tongs, carried the ice in and put it in your ice box. Refrigerators came along fairly soon, of course, but I still savor the memories of the kids in the neighborhood running up to the ice wagon, reaching in and getting to eat the little chips of ice that fell when the ice was cut. I fear that the children of today will never have those kinds of summertime memories.

There were also a number of farmers who lived in the county who were peddlers. Usually they had small buggies or wagons. They had what we would call a truck farm today. In the spring they would cultivate lettuce and peas and beans and onions and okra and tomatoes and all the wide variety of garden vegetables that we have today. Whatever they had that had come to maturity at that particular time they would load into their wagons and they would come through town. Most had regular routes. I remember a man named Richie Floyd, who I think lived down past the Tarwater stretch, who would always stop at our house and come to the door and tell my mother what he had that day.

Mr. Floyd didn't waste his words. He came to the door and he said, "I got green beans. I got green onions. I got carrots. I got taters."

Mother would then say, "Well, Mr. Floyd, if your beans are real nice bring me a gallon of your green beans and a bunch of your green onions." Mr. Floyd had no scales, so he measured by quarts, gallons, pecks or bushels, and that's the way the business was transacted.

One of the most popular things in Sevier County, and I suppose throughout the South, is cornbread. I have always been a student of cornbread because I have always loved it. It's interesting to me that the recipes for cornbread vary tremendously. During the days when I was growing up, every housewife had her own way to make cornbread, and each family generally liked the way their mother or wife made cornbread and didn't like the way anybody else made it.

There were a lot of different types of cornbread. Some people would use cornmeal and buttermilk, and maybe add some flour, sugar, and eggs. It would almost have a cake texture and sweet taste. Some people used yellow cornmeal, and some white. The more Puritan type made the bread with white cornmeal, milk, lard and maybe an egg. This was the purest kind of cornbread.

There were two ways to serve cornbread. You were either a "breaker" or a "cutter." Some people cut their cornbread, usually into pie-like triangles from a round pan. In this way, each person got a piece. But the real Puritans believed that cutting the cornbread did something bad to the taste and you were supposed to break the cornbread into pieces. My father always told me that we were breakers.

Of course, one popular way to eat cornbread, especially at the end of the meal if you were still a little hungry and there was cornbread left, was to take a big glass of sweet milk and crumble up the cornbread in the milk and eat it with a spoon. Believe me, that's a very, very good way to eat cornbread. But I still think there's nothing better than some hot cornbread and butter, either pinto beans or soup beans, and a big, sweet Vidalia onion.

Making molasses in Sevier County when I was growing up was really a community event. Families would pool together to make molasses because it was too big an operation for each family to make their own. Sometimes the whole community would be involved in the making of molasses.

The cane was grown and harvested in the fall and cut into stalks that were stacked up at the place where the molasses would be made. The molasses mill consisted of two large rollers that mashed up the cane, a pan underneath to catch the juice, and a long, stout pole extending outward to a track. A horse would be hitched to the far end of the pole and would make a circle around the mill on the worn track. As the horse pushed the pole around, the pole powered the grinder (the two rollers). The cane stalks were fed into the masher and, as the two big rollers turned, they pulled the cane through between them. This squeezed out the juice, which dripped into the big pan at the bottom. The juice, which was green and really kind of awful looking, was taken to a big metal vat sitting over a fire. People took turns standing by the vat with a skimmer, skimming off a residue that made the molasses bitter, until the syrup was just right. Then the molasses was bottled.

It is a true delicacy to pour molasses into your plate, mix into it a good hunk of butter, and put it on a hot biscuit. I don't remember anything much better than that!

MONDAY WAS WASHDAY

Way before the time of washing machines, especially the automatic machines that are everywhere today, every house had a wash house in an outbuilding, little more than a roof and walls, sometimes with a floor and sometimes not. Inside were long wooden tables where the wash tubs were kept. The tables were low so the person doing the wash could bend over the tubs with a wash board and scrub the clothes. Then there were other tubs with rinse water, then the clothes were wrung out by hand and hung up on a clothes line outside the building. In addition, there was a wash kettle, usually outside the wash house, set up on bricks or stones so a fire could be built underneath. In many instances the clothes were washed by being boiled in this kettle. At our home my father had built what was considered to be a pretty nice wash house. It was made of brick, on the south end of the garage. There were two rooms behind the garage. One was the smokehouse, and the other was the wash house. Our wash house had a concrete floor and there was a furnace door on the outside wall with the wash kettle set in concrete inside, so that you went outside to build the fire and it heated the water in the kettle.

Mother usually had two women come to wash on Monday. Much of the time she had roomers in the house, so there was a considerable amount of clothes to wash, and she always prided herself on the fact that she kept a clean, white shirt for my father to wear every day. This meant seven shirts had to be washed and ironed, a pretty good task in itself. One reason you always knew when it was Monday and wash day was that lunch was very simple, usually soup beans and cornbread and, of course, milk. This was a lunch that I didn't enjoy as much then as I should have because today I consider soup beans and cornbread and a big, sweet onion a very fine meal indeed. Generally Tuesday's lunch included chicken hash. Often Mother would fix a hen or some sort of chicken on Sunday. Because of wash day on Monday, she didn't have time to pick the bones and carcass of that hen, so she did it on Tuesday.

About 1937 or 1938, my father made a big trade, at least very big for our family. At that time he was in the automobile business selling Chrysler-Plymouth automobiles and International trucks. A fairly new hardware store had opened down on the square. Crumb DeLozier and his partner were operating this store and my father traded them a new International pickup truck for an electric stove and an easy washing machine with a spin chamber, rather than a wringer, to partially dry the clothes before they were hung out. Also in the deal was a Kelvinator electric refrigerator and an ironer that was known as a mangle. It had a big, round pad and heat came off the top and you could run sheets and things like that through the mangle.

This certainly changed the way my mother functioned as a cook and housekeeper in our home. Obviously, the wash was made much simpler, even though the washing machine was put out in the wash house and stayed out there, as I recall, for several years. The mangle was very handy for her because she would run sheets and large, flat items through the mangle. And the Kelvinator refrigerator was a real improvement over the old ice box with the ice man coming each day. The electric stove was also a very nice addition. It had a feature on it which, as far as I know, is not used any more. It was called a deep well cooker. It went down into the range, and Mother cooked some awfully fine beans and vegetables in that deep well cooker.

WHEN WINTER CAME

Winter was a fun time in Sevierville. One of the things that we always looked forward to when winter came, usually near Thanksgiving, was hog killing time. This usually came in November, because you wanted a pretty cold day so the meat wouldn't spoil. The first frosts usually come in this area around the second week in October.

Almost every family had a hog to be killed. They might have some place where they would fatten the hog themselves, a hog pen, or they might have a friend or relative that would fatten their hog on a farm. They might even buy the hog. This was a time for a lot of social activity because family and friends would get together to help. The process started when a large, black wash kettle was brought to the site and filled with water and a fire built to provide hot water. The hog was killed by hitting it in the head with an ax or shooting it with a twenty-two. It was then hoisted up by its hind legs under a tree or a beam in the barn. The hog was cut open and the intestines and so forth carefully removed. Then the hog was butchered into hams and shoulders and tenderloin. The kettle was then used to render the lard. The fat and trimmings were put into the kettle and lard was rendered out and put in five-gallon lard cans that you bought at the store. This was the cooking oil of the early days and I'm amazed at how, today, that is looked down on as a fattening and dangerous way to cook because of the high cholesterol and heart problems it can lead to. But during that time lard was used for baking and cooking by most families and cooking oils were generally unknown. When the lard was rendered, the very dry crust, what was left of the meat and fat that had been put into the kettle, was called cracklins. These were crisp and some people considered them a delicacy. They did taste pretty good. They also made awfully good dog food. The dogs really loved the cracklins.

Another product from the hogs was sausage. The meat was trimmed and generally taken to a store, where it was ground into sausage. It was preserved in several ways. Sometimes it was cooked and placed in Bell canning jars. My mother sewed out of cloth a long, tubular sack and the sausage was stuffed into the sack and hung up in the smokehouse. You sliced it off in round, sausage patties.

The hams were salted down for a number of days in the smokehouse. Everybody had their own recipe for pepper and other spices that were rubbed on over the salt. Then the hams were hung up in bags to cure into country ham, which was considered the main delicacy of the hog. The shoulders were generally cut into roasts or just sliced and eaten like the ham.

My father would sometimes kill two or three hogs and this meat was given to my grandmother, uncles and aunts, and others. Dad was always very careful when we killed hogs to send a mess of the fresh meat, some of the backbone and ribs, some of the tenderloin, some of the sausage, to all the preachers in the town. His father had been a preacher and he felt like preachers were not paid very much in those days. So every preacher — Methodist, Baptist, Presbyterian and any other church in town — a mess of fresh meat when we killed hogs. My brother or I would get on our bicycles and deliver that meat.

It is strange how some things you did as a child stick indelibly in your mind. I recall vividly my father always saying, "Be sure and don't miss that Methodist preacher. Those Methodists never have paid their preacher enough to get along on and he's going to need it."

I've told that story to several Methodist preacher friends and I don't recall ever having a single Methodist preacher disagree with that statement.

CARS

Cars were a very important part of growing up in Sevierville during my youth. When World War II came along there were no automobiles manufactured for domestic use from 1941 until 1946, so the car you had when the war started was the car that got you through the war. As you can imagine, there was a real shortage of cars and it took a couple of years for everybody to get a new car after the war. For our family, my dad ended up with a 1941 Plymouth. He had been in the automobile business prior to that time with J. B. Waters Motor Company, and later the Rector-Waters Motor Company in partnership with Mr. Jim Rector. As I previously mentioned, he had the Chrysler-Plymouth agency for a few years and also sold International trucks. Mr. Rector had the Dodge agency. All these were Chrysler products, so they merged and operated together until the war came along and Mr. Rector's death. I remember they got a few 1942 cars that were sent to the company, but the government confiscated those cars before any were sold. They were taken away for use in the war. The Chrysler Motor Company, along with General Motors and Ford and other motor companies, all converted to making tanks, various engines for tanks and war craft, trucks and Jeeps and all the vehicles that were needed for the war effort.

Horse-drawn wagons and buggies were still quite common in Sevierville during those early days and, I suppose, because of the war you saw more and more of them. A lot of grain, corn and wheat was brought into the mills by horse-drawn wagon. I have heard it discussed that before my recollection Sevierville had quite an interesting distinction. The fastest overland, horse-drawn stage in American supposedly ran from Sevierville to Knoxville. The horses pulled a stagecoach similar to the ones seen in the movies. The horses ran all the way and were changed some four or five times between Sevierville and Knoxville, because the horses couldn't run the whole twenty-five miles. One of the places they changed horses was at Rocky Springs in Boyd's Creek, now owned by the Temple family. There was a house there where people could get on and off when the stage stopped. The stagecoach carried mail as well.

One of Sevierville's early courthouses was down at what was then the public square. Adjacent to the public square over on the East Prong was a lot known as the Jockey Lot. This was one of the places where people coming in from rural sections could tie up their horses. It was also a place where a lot of horse trading took place. My father told me there was a post at the Jockey Lot, where, if you had a horse you didn't want and you were willing to trade him for any other horse, you tied him to that post. If a man came along with a horse he liked less than your horse, he would tie his horse up to the post and take yours. These were obviously not desirable horses.

My father was quite a horseman. He knew horses very, very well and was an expert at handling horses. I always loved horses and I regretted that he didn't teach me more about horses, but he was not a very good teacher.

When my father ran for Circuit Court Clerk in 1910, he campaigned on horseback. He wasn't married then and he lived in the Snaphouse Hotel, which had a stable behind it. During that campaign he got horses to use by agreeing to break and train hard-to-handle horses for people. When he rode a horse every day into the rural sections on hard rides, the horse would pretty quickly get so the owners could handle him while providing Dad with free transportation.

However, at the end of the election he had a serious accident. He had a horse that was an outlaw, a difficult horse. He was tied up in the stall behind the Snaphouse Hotel. When my father went to feed the horse one afternoon, the horse kicked him in the head and knocked him unconscious and probably would have killed him, except that a Deputy United States Marshal happened to be walking through the stable at that time and grabbed my father's foot and pulled him out. He was unconscious for days before recovering. In the meantime, he had been elected Circuit Court Clerk and while he was unconscious some friends had to make his bond for office. He had a crease on the top of his head all his life and his friends and my mother would occasionally make joking references to the fact he had gotten kicked in the head.

I mentioned that automobiles were very important. My grandfather, A. M. Paine, always drove a Buick in those days. One of the best cars in town was one owned by Mr. S. L. Atchley, the cashier of Sevier County Bank. His car was a LaSalle. This was an automobile made by General Motors for a few years. This was considered to be a very fine car. I remember when the war ended after 1945 and cars were made again after 1946, that C. Earl Ogle, who lived in Gatlinburg, got the first Cadillac brought into Sevier County after World War II. It was quite a sight to see. People would go just to look at it. Other people in Gatlinburg began to buy expensive cars like that and there was a story out that you had to owe more than a hundred thousand dollars before you were qualified to buy a Cadillac.

I think I learned to drive around the age of thirteen. Dad had been in the automobile business prior to that time, and I would go down and start the cars and try to move them around in the area where they were parked beside the building. J. B. Waters Motor Company was just next door to where we lived at 107 Joy Street. The motor company was at the corner of Court Avenue and Joy Street. So I learned to start and stop cars pretty early on and, like any young lad, I wanted a car. Wheels were very important to anybody, but the war was on and it was a tough time.

When I got to be fourteen years old, my friend, Bud Reno, told me, "If you want to get your driver's license, go over to the courthouse on the day that highway patrolman comes up there to give the tests. He's awful lenient. If you tell him you're sixteen years old, he'll let you take the test and give you a driver's license."

I was only fourteen, but the temptation was too great and I succumbed and committed that lie. I went over and told the man that I was sixteen, he gave me the test and I got my license. So, of course, I needed transportation. The motor company garage had been closed when war came in 1942 and they couldn't get any more cars, and back in the corner was the last vehicle my father had used in the operation of the Sunnyside Dairy Farm. This was a 1933 Dodge panel truck. It had a door in the back and two bucket seats up front. It had been used to deliver milk until the dairy was closed when World War II started. The dairy was no longer a really profitable operation. The Yett family had a much larger dairy operation in the county then and they were the first people in the county to pasteurize milk.

But there sat this old panel truck in the back of the garage with all kind of boxes and old tires and junk piled around it. I asked Mel Watson, who had been a mechanic there, what was wrong with that old panel truck.

Mel said, "Well, I don't think there's much wrong with it. As I remember, the fuel pump's bad on it."

I said, "How do you get that fixed?"

"Well," he said, "go down to the Western Auto and for twelve dollars you can buy a kit to rebuild a fuel pump and I'll show you how to do that."

So I did. We rebuilt the fuel pump, pumped the tires, charged the battery and, lo and behold, the vehicle started! All of a sudden I had wheels. I drove that panel truck around town and to the Pine Grove swimming hole when we went up there to swim, and used it for a long time. One of the main problems with the truck was the fact that the left door, the driver's door, didn't work well, so I managed that by just taking the door off. It was easy to get in and out of the truck without the door anyway.

It had two bucket seats, and I well remember that the passenger's bucket seat was not bolted down right to the floor and it was kind of loose. Generally everybody that rode with me knew about that, but one day I was coming up Main Street near the library when my mother came out of the library. I stopped and picked her up to take her home. She got in and sat down and I started off a little too fast and that bucket seat turned over into the back. My mother turned a flip over into the back of the panel truck. Fortunately, she wasn't hurt, but I bolted that seat down after that.

My friends and I got a lot of pleasure out of riding in that old truck. It had various mechanical problems, but we were usually able to patch it up and keep it going. After they built and opened Douglas Dam and would allow you to fish out there — I think you could fish in 1942 — we'd go out in the old panel truck to fish. One day we were out there fishing and we stayed a little later than we intended to and it got dark. My brother David and his wife, Ina, had a boat out there and we were using the boat to fish in. Bud Reno, my friend, was with us. We started to come home and found that the fuel pump had gone out. The only light that would burn on the truck was the dome light overhead, so we realized we were in a bad situation, but we had to get home. We raised the hood on the car and my brother sat on the fender. Bud Reno had a five-gallon can of gasoline that we used for the motor boat and a Coke bottle. The way we drove the car was, Bud stood on the running board with a five-gallon can of gas, emptied the Coke bottle and filled it up out of the five-gallon can, handed it to my brother who poured it down into the carburetor with the air filter off. I was at the wheel and drove, but because of the way they sat on the running board of the fender, I had to look out the side where the door had been to see, and Ina sat in the driver's seat and held the floor shift in gear, because if you didn't hold it down it would jump out of gear. When we saw a car either approaching or about to overtake us, since we had no lights, we pulled to the side of the road, stopped and turned on the dome light so the other car could see us and safely get by us. That's the way we drove the panel truck back to Sevierville. Because the motorboat gasoline had oil in it, we laid a heavy fog of smoke from the lake to Sevierville, but we arrived safely.

Later on I sold that Dodge panel truck to a man in town for $75. He didn't have any money and I made a bad mistake and took his note. He never paid me. I employed Mr. O. M. Connatser, a very fine attorney in town, to sue him but the effort was unsuccessful. The buyer wrote Mr. Connatser a letter and told him that I had fed him a "lion" about that vehicle and he wasn't going to pay it ... and he didn't.

My next vehicle was a 1929 A-Model Ford. David, my brother, had saved up enough money and we bought it for about $300. I was in high school and it was a very popular way to get back and forth to school. Later I traded that for a 1930 A-Model Ford, which was a little bit better car. These were two-door sedans with a back seat. My friends and I really enjoyed that vehicle. I would drive it home from high school for lunch and after lunch I went back to school. Generally, when I came out the door of 107 Joy Street, seated in the front seat was Patsy Temple, who lived just around the corner on Court Avenue: she wanted a ride back to school. Jack Snapp, who lived just up the street, would usually be in the car as well and we would pick up anyone else we saw along the way.

These A-Model Fords were very fine automobiles that Mr. Ford manufactured after he was able to make vast improvements on what he called the T-Model. This Ford had two levers on either side of the steering wheel. One was the spark, which would advance the spark on the engine. The other was the throttle. If the car was in good shape — and I kept this car in good shape — you put what they called "both ears" (the levers) up and the spark was very low and the car would idle with a neat kind of sound, "Chug, chug,

chug" and we called that "Cadillac-ing" through town. That's the way we circled through town on a Saturday afternoon.

The A-Model had one feature that was not a smart thing to do, but young as I was, I was not above doing it. I would drive along the road where people walked. If I was going a pretty good speed, twenty-five or thirty miles an hour, and turned the ignition off, pumped the accelerator about two times, then turn the ignition switch back on, the car would make a loud backfire that sounded a lot like a shotgun. We were not above doing this to scare people and call attention to ourselves. One time I recall Mr. Ledwell, the high school principal, telling me he didn't want to hear that Ford backfire any more and I had to limit that activity.

THE SEVIER COUNTY FAIR

Each year at Labor Day the Sevier County Fair brought to the fairground a midway as well as exhibits where farmers and other people bring in their products, livestock, displays, crafts and art work. It has always been a big week in the county and still is today.

The fair was organized in 1935 and my father, J. B. Waters, was the first president of the fair. I was six years old at the time and for a number of years after that the coming of the fair was just about one of the biggest things that happened in Sevier County. There were exhibits and judging of all kinds of livestock including cattle, horses, pigs, and chickens, and that time we had a Sevier County Horse Show in conjunction with the fair, although we haven't had a horse show with the fair for several years now. In the exhibit hall women would bring in samples of their canned goods, bakery products, sewing and knitting, and all kinds of crafts and arts.

The big part of the fair for a kid was the midway. The midway had the rides, sideshows and games and other activities that traveled from town to town. The midway that I recall the most was owned by a man from over in Maryville in Blount County. His name was Shan Wilcox, but the name of his show was Shan Brothers Shows and it always amused me because Mr. Wilcox didn't have a brother. There were many things on the midway other than the rides. There were the little games such as shooting galleries where you could win prizes, just like in the midways of today.

A big event in the midway back then was the wrestling tent. The people with the show set up their tent with a ring in the middle of it. The crowd paid to get in the tent and just stood around the ring. There was always a wrestler who travelled with the show. He was always a big, strong-looking man and usually played the part of the mean guy. Back in those days local wrestlers would challenge the travelling wrestler and put on a show. In my childhood we had two Sevier County men who were kind of semi-professional wrestlers and pretty well known in the area. One was a man named Barefoot Ballard, who got his name from wrestling barefoot. The other was named Sailor Clark. Both were popular with Sevier County audiences and usually wrestled the mean guy who came with the show.

One year I remember particularly well. There was a big, big, mean, tough-looking guy who came with the show and he really knew how to put on the bad guy act. After a lot of preliminary bouts were held, Sailor Clark was going to wrestle. I paid to get in to this event, where a large crowd had gathered.

We had a local gentleman in town, Mr. Sam Isenburg, who was the owner of the Ford dealership in Sevierville, although his sons did most of the work running the business. Mr. Isenburg was always a well-dressed man, wearing a three-piece suit, generally gray, and a nice hat, and carrying a walking stick.

I was standing at a corner of the ring beside Mr. Isenburg watching the match. As it progressed, Sailor Clark was really getting the bad end of the match. He was getting treated pretty badly by the mean guy. Suddenly, the bad guy came near the corner of the ring where we were standing and Mr. Isenburg took his walking stick, held it by the far end, and reached in with the crooked handle and tripped the mean guy as he went by.

The huge wrestler hit the mat pretty hard, jumped up and started pointing and hollering, "This man tripped me! He tripped me!" He looked at me and asked, "Did you see this man trip me?"

I looked up at him and answered, "Mister, I didn't see a thing!"

I've mentioned that unusual, weird and strange things came into Sevierville with the Sevier County Fair through the midway. One event which happened about 1939 or 1940 was certainly a surprise to me.

A man was seen living in the Central Hotel, and questions arose among us boys about his identity. Well, the answer was that he had something to do with the midway at the fair, but he rented a room in the Central Hotel instead of staying at the fairgrounds with the rest of the midway people.

This itself was a little bit unusual, because the midway was pretty well self-contained. They had their house trailers, campers and tents and usually lived right on site. But this person, who looked a little unusual anyway, was living at the hotel. Our curiosity was finally satisfied when we found out that, in one of the strange sideshows at the midway, he was the hermaphrodite.

Now I had no idea what this was, but Joe DeLozier, who had commenced to study medicine even at that early age, enlightened me.

You had paid twenty-five cents to get into the tent, but after you got in and saw a short show, you had to pay another fifty cents to go into a back room to see both parts of the show. We were used to seeing all kinds of fraudulent things at the fair, and this one was a surprise and shock, because, sure enough, it was so!

Certainly an awful lot of the events and side shows were not true, but were just little curiosity things that the promoters had thought up and the barkers would sell. One that caught my fancy had a great barker out front. He always told his story like this:

"Step right up, folks. Come right over here. See Alice, the Alligator Girl ... and her alive! She neither walks or talks, but craw-wals upon her belly like a reptile. Step right up, folks. See Alice, the Alligator Girl. Only twenty-five cents ... one quarter of a dollar. Alice, the Alligator Girl ... step right up."

A.M. Paine, JBW maternal grandfather.

J.B. Waters, Sr. ... "The High Command" ... made at age 70.

Dad and Mother at their 50th Wedding Anniversary.

THE CONNECTION

I am amused at the name some people use to identify their family. A large family I know always refers to the family group as "the clan." Others may use "the tribe" or "the kin." Some even use the term "Mafia" as a collective name for their family. My father's Grandfather Myers always referred to "the connection" as the collective name for his relatives. In letters to friends who lived elsewhere he would state that the health of the connection "is all generally well except Cousin Sara, who is poorly." My Aunt Zora titled her book on the family The Connection in East Tennessee. We don't know too much about the Waterses. A man named Enoch Waters married Elizabeth Wear, daughter of Colonel Samuel Wear. Wear was a very early settler of Sevier County. He was a friend of John Sevier and served as a captain under John Sevier at Kings Mountain.

It always seemed to me that we were told about those in the family who did well, were successful or possessed special talents. The ones that did not do well or got into any trouble we flat just did not talk about. Occasionally a relation would take me aside and in a low whisper tell the bad news about one of the connection.

My Grandfather Paine was over in North Carolina one time in an area where he knew that a number of Paines had lived. He saw a sign "Paine's Store". He went in the store and ask the clerk if Mr. Paine was in. "No," the clerk replied. "Paine is in the penitentiary." Grandfather left without further inquiry.

My earliest memories all center on our home at 107 Joy Street. The radius of my activities, measured from that center, was a very short distance.

Our mother was the person in charge. Dad got up, left, and in general came and went. Mother was always there. As I now look back and recollect, she was a very efficient and well-organized person. Her day was spent in the time-consuming work of the mother and housewife, but our home was more than the typical household. Three of the seven bedrooms were rented to roomers who paid Mother for the rent of the room by the month. She never took a "boarder," one to whom she served meals. In the summer months the house became the Joy Street Tourist Home and we had overnight guests.

In addition to the boarding roomers and tourists, our house was Dad's office. It was only one block to the courthouse and the downtown section. People looking for Dad for business purposes came to the house. We very seldom knew were he was; however, we could inform them that he would be home for the next meal. Consequently, it was not unusual for people to knock on the door during dinner or supper. I never recall Dad getting up from the table to meet them. Mother or one of us went to the door and told them to have a seat, that he would be out soon. The front porch was used as a waiting room during the summer.

Dad was an independent businessman, a one-man show. He disliked appointments or schedules and came, went, bought and sold, and spent his day seemingly on impulse. He was a "gut" trader. Before he bought a farm, a house, or a mule, he saw every fault. After he traded, he saw only good qualities. He was the most positive thinking man I ever knew. He had full confidence in his own ability. He was quick to anger and criticize. However, after saying exactly what he thought, he was just as quick to put the matter aside and forget it. He had a remarkable memory, especially in regard to people and real estate. He could almost give a recitation on the chain of title on every major piece of property in Sevier County. He believed that real estate was the basis of all wealth.

I spent many hours riding with him in the car as he went about trading and doing business. He could do many things that I, as a young boy, wanted to learn; however, he was a poor teacher. He did not have the patience to teach me how to handle and crack a black snake whip, how to shoot a gun, or very little of his amazing knowledge of horses. I did learn some by observation.

Dad's academic education was very limited. He read and used the English language very well. His writing was not so good. He knew very little grammar, and his spelling was poor. The latter fault is one that I inherited.

He was indeed a remarkable man. He enjoyed life, never worried, and considered himself totally self-sufficient. Pete Hailey, his son-in-law, referred to him as the "High Command," a title we all adopted and one that indeed fit.

Dad enjoyed very good health. He told us that as a child he was sick a lot and was not very strong. However, he was very strong and healthy as an adult. He said his role model was Theodore Roosevelt, who also was a sickly child but grew up to be a strong adult. In 1919 there was a flu epidemic in the country. Dad caught the flu. Mother said that was the only time he was in bed sick during their marriage. I never saw him in bed sick until just weeks before his death in 1976. He liked to boast that he could hold all the pills he had ever taken in the palms of his hands. We used to laugh and say that disease would not dare strike him.

As a young boy, however, there was no place where I felt as safe as at my mother's side. She offered total security, and she encouraged me to excel in a way that only mothers can. She was such a strong, stable person, always consistent, that I took her far too much for granted. I was grown long before I realized what an unusual woman she really was.

Her goal in life was to be an efficient housewife and mother. She prepared herself for these duties and she did them well. Mother was an excellent cook and an excellent housekeeper. Our home, as I have mentioned, was well managed. I never saw her in the morning in a robe or not fully dressed. She got up first, before anyone else. She always wore a clean, pretty housedress and was always neat. Her hair was auburn, usually short and always pretty and well combed. She had excellent posture (the only one in the family who did), stood and walked very straight and with beautiful dignity. Dignified is perhaps the best word to describe her. She did everything with dignity. When Mother died, Mary Louise said that she died with dignity.

Mother was a strong person. When she felt strong about an issue, she did not hesitate to take action. Unlike Dad, however, she did not belabor the point. She just got the job done.

I was told that in 1920 when the Women's Suffrage was at issue, she campaigned very hard for the Right of Women to Vote. She promoted rallies and parades in support of the issue, even though both her father and Dad were not supporters.

The thirties were bad times. Many were out of work and some did not have enough to eat. Many came to Mother's back door and asked for food. She never turned anyone away. She used to laugh and say that she thought there was a mark on our house which told these people that they could get food there.

There was a special group of men who lived in town that she was very fond of. These men were her former students. Many of them had her for their first teacher. It was easy to identify these men as they called her "Miss Myrtle." They tipped their hats when she passed them on the street.

Mother had a different relationship with each of us children. She and Mary Louise enjoyed the full mother-daughter relationship. They had long talks, which seemed to me at the time endless and went into great detail over all of Mary Louise's activities. However, she did not pry. It seemed that Mary Louise wanted to tell her everything she did in school or in social activities. I remember being a little envious of their relationship but unable to understand what they had to talk about for so long. David required special attention. It seemed that Mother had to be constantly alert to keep up with him and knowledgeable of his activities. Indeed, she loved us all. In our own way, we each wanted to please her with our conduct.

I knew only one set of my grandparents, my mother's parents. The Waters grandparents both died before I was born. I think it's very important for people to have grandparents and I feel sorry for anyone who never knew their grandparents. A grandmother is a person who can always support you, always be on your side, even when you're wrong and can love you in a way that no one else can. The parents do have the responsibility of correcting and disciplining, whereas most grandmothers can just be totally on your side.

That was certainly true of my Grandmother Paine. Her name was Susie Watson and she was in many ways a country woman. She was not real well educated, but she was a very determined woman when she wanted to be. Quilting was her hobby. She was a good cook but not a fancy cook, and her housekeeping was not the most important thing in her life. She wanted to get through with those tasks so she could quilt. She always had a nice vegetable garden and she always had her chickens for eggs. I loved my grandmother very much and going to see her was a very special thing in my life.

They lived only a couple of blocks up from where I was born, so we visited there quite often.

My grandfather, Ambrose Miller Paine, was a very dominant male in our family. He was a most unusual man and a man that I admired very, very much. I was seventeen years old when he died on September 20, 1947, which was the same day that I enrolled as a freshman in the University of Tennessee.

Grandfather was a lawyer and had, at one time, been a circuit judge, and he was known all over this section of the country as Judge Paine. Almost everyone called him Judge Paine. A few old friends of his he had known for years called him Ambers. To me he was Papaw. He was born in North Carolina one year after the Civil War ended. It must have been a terribly tough time in the South during those years. The economy was devastated, the land had been misused or not used at all, farming was extremely difficult. It's hard for me to contemplate how really poor and difficult the times were then to live and raise a family and just simply have enough to eat. It was described by many people as "hard times," and I think indeed it must have been hard times.

My grandfather's father, Smith Ferguson Paine, had served in the Confederate Army and been in the State of Tennessee as a Confederate soldier in a number of battles. After the war ended he returned to his home in Swain County, North Carolina, and my grandfather, A. M. Paine, was the first child born. Things were so difficult during those days that in 1886 Smith Ferguson Paine sold his farm and what he had over in North Carolina and came across the mountain to East Tennessee. My grandfather was twenty years old then. I remember hearing him and father talk about how difficult it was to "scratch out a living," as it was called, on the Knob Farm that they bought about four miles east of Gatlinburg in what was then called the Shady Grove Community. The farm was on Bird's Creek and had a little creek bottom, but it also had a lot of upland where they tried to grow corn and other crops.

The difficulties in getting an education were almost insurmountable. There were very, very few schools and what schools were available (sometimes called subscription schools where parents would hire a teacher and make a pot of money to pay them) would sometimes last three weeks or maybe longer. Grandfather recognized early on the value of an education and whereever he could find a school, or hear about a school in a community nearby or at least close enough that he walked to get to, he would go and try to enroll and learn what he could.

I recall him telling me that he was twenty-one years old before he ever learned that there was such a thing as fractions, any number smaller than one. He said this fascinated him and he kept asking teachers if they knew about fractions. A friend named Z. D. Massey had come across the mountain with the Paines and had gone on into Sevierville. Grandfather heard that there was a school over in what was known as Pine Grove, near Pigeon Forge, that had just opened and that the teacher might be able to teach fractions. This was about ten miles from Grandfather's home, but he walked over there. He walked in the schoolhouse, which happened to be in session when he arrived, and there at the front of the class, teaching the class, was his friend Massey. He immediately was concerned about whether or not he had made a wise trip and he asked, "Massey, do you know anything about fractions?"

To which Massey replied, "Ambers ... fractions ... what does that mean?"

My grandfather replied, "It means that I walked ten miles for nothing."

Strangely enough, Massey later became a physician and was a prominent medical doctor in Sevier County for a number of years. He later served a short term in the Congress of the United States from the First Congressional District.

In any event, Grandfather made every effort to educate himself. He talked about how little he knew and how little he was able to find out. One day he was grubbing sprouts on the side of the hill on the family farm with his father. He told me he stuck his mattock in a stump and told his daddy that there must be a better way to make a living and he was going to go into town and see if he couldn't better himself. His father apparently understood his decision and did not object to it. He told him, "Well, we'll hitch up the wagon and I'll take you to Hodson's Ford and set you across the river and you can walk the rest of the way."

Hodson's Ford was near what today is still known as Hodson's Bridge on the East Prong of the Little Pigeon River where the road forks to go to Pitman Center. This is the route they came, down the East Prong to the Hodson Place. He walked the rest of the way into Sevierville. He told me that he had a few clothes and twenty-five cents in money. He came into Sevierville and with no better place to go, he went to the Sevier County Jail, which was then located in the Public Square. He was fortunate enough to get a job as turnkey. He kept the keys to the jail and put the prisoners in and let them out by order of the sheriff. This served him to good advantage because he had a place to sleep and he could eat out of the jail kitchen which served the prisoners. He began to get acquainted around town and immediately became interested in the law.

There were a number of lawyers in town then. Mr. George Zirkle, General Pickle and Mr. James Royal Penland were practicing in Sevierville at that time and my grandfather spent a lot of time with Mr. Penland. Mr. Penland was an influential man in helping him become a lawyer.

During this time he at least got back up on Bird's Creek occasionally and in 1890 married my grandmother, Susie Watson, who lived three miles down the creek from the Paine place. Her father was David Corn Watson, and it's interesting to note that he had been a Union soldier. So this united two families, one headed by a former Confederate soldier and the other by a former Union soldier.

The Watson family was apparently more prosperous than the Paine family because they were known to have plenty to eat and a good place to live. They had a large family and my grandfather would go there to court Susie. My grandfather was still pretty poor after they were married and they had to stay with her family. My mother was born at the Watson home about a year after they were married.

In addition to reading law, Grandfather made every effort he could to further his general education, attending classes at Murphy College and at one time going down for a term at Chilhowee Academy. In general he always did whatever he could to further his academic education.

In March, 1895, he was admitted to the bar and commenced to practice law. He worked a lot with General Penland and they formed a partnership. He was a very industrious, hard-working man and it didn't take him long to be a successful lawyer. He then brought the family to Sevierville and they lived in a little old house on Cedar Street across the street from the Methodist Church. Pretty soon just a few hundred feet up Park Road he bought a small house on the west side of the road where they lived for several years.

In 1898 he felt as if he still needed to have a better legal education, even though he had been admitted to the Bar and had been practicing law for four years. So he saved up enough money to go to Knoxville and he enrolled in the University of Tennessee College of Law. The College of Law then was a two-year course, but he took the two-year course in one year. He told me later that his goal while he was down there was to read a hundred pages of law a day, and that was the way he measured his progress as a student. He worked very hard and he had very little to live on while he was there. He rented a cheap room, and one time he literally ran out of food and had only a very little bit of money and was concerned about how he was going to survive. He really didn't have enough money to continue a proper diet. He made a unique decision. He bought a dozen fresh eggs, five pounds of sugar and a gallon of white moonshine whiskey. He said you can take a glass of whiskey and cut it down with a little water, put a raw egg in it with several spoonfuls of sugar, and he said there was quite a bit of energy there. That was one way he survived studying law. He graduated from the University of Tennessee Law School, and of course returned to Sevierville.

His practice grew immensely. In 1901 he was elected the first mayor of the City of Sevierville, as it had just become incorporated. As his practice grew he bought property when he could, if he had a few dollars or could borrow it. He organized Sevier County Bank in 1909 and served on its board as attorney and later president of the bank until his death. He was very interested in the bank. The other bank in town was what was known as the old bank, or the Bank of Sevierville.

Papaw told an interesting story. They were living in the little house on the west side of Park Road and he bought a very nice lot almost directly across the street and commenced to build a new house over there, a much nicer, larger, two-story home. But he told Susie that he thought they couldn't afford to move over there and live in the new house, that he would have to sell the house when they got it finished. But Susie watched them construct that house and she wanted to move in it regardless of what he said. Since she just lived across the street from it, she observed the construction as it went on. My grandfather got up every morning and walked the four or five blocks from home to his office, which was upstairs over the Sevier County Bank Building. The house was nearing completion and one morning he got up and walked to his office. While he was gone Susie went across the street to the carpenters who were finishing up in the new house and had them move all the furniture across the street into the new home. My grandfather used to laugh when he told this story. He would say that she had carpenters put poles under the edge of the stove and literally moved the cook stove with fire in it to the new house. When noon came he walked home and turned to step up on the porch of the old house. She was on the porch across the street and she hollered at him and said, "We're having dinner over here today."

After that he bought and built a number of houses. He would say, "Well, I bought a house up in Frog Alley last night. I don't know whether Susie will move up there or not."

He had lived such a poor life and they had very little when he grew up as a child. My mother told me that his mother (her grandmother) was a very poor cook, but she was a great gardener and they had beautiful flowers. She would sit out in the yard and read poetry, but there was very little to eat in the house. Mother said when they were going up to visit later on the children always wanted to eat at the Watson family house instead of at the Paine family house. But after my grandfather became more successful, he did not want to live that way any more. He had a number of likes and dislikes and he was an opinionated man, to say the least. He refused to eat in the kitchen. He wanted to have his meals in the dining room and the new house had a dining room. And he insisted on eating on a white linen table cloth with white linen napkins. He also refused to eat cornbread. Cornbread is a very popular bread and still is today in our family. But my mother said that the reason Grandfather didn't like cornbread was that his mother couldn't make cornbread fit to eat and so he refused to eat it. My grandmother made biscuits three times a day because Grandfather loved biscuits.

Papaw had a number of other peculiarities that amused me. He built a large, concrete tank reservoir in the back of the house where he captured all the rain water that came off this rather large house. Into the bathroom was piped hot and cold well water and hot and cold rain water out of the tank. Of course, rain water was much softer and he would bathe only in rain water. It was kind of a popular place. My mother used to tell me that there were a number of her girl friends who loved to come up to their house and wash their hair because of the very nice, soft rain water. Our well water and city water were much harder, and still are today for that matter.

Papaw wore a navy blue serge suit and a black, string bow tie and a black Stetson hat with no crease in the crown. He ordered these suits tailor made, two and three at a time, and he would order hats two and three at a time. Mr. Ed Shepard, a friend in the mercantile business then, ordered his clothes. He was always fearful of running out so he bought underwear, handkerchiefs, socks, and apparel like that by the dozen. He did occasionally in the summer have a white linen suit for very hot weather. This was in the days before any air conditioning. In the summertime, when July came and it got hot, he got up early and went to his office and worked until noon or shortly before noon, came home and had his lunch or what they called dinner then — you ate breakfast, dinner and supper in those days. And then he went to a big white rocking chair under the trees in his yard and occasionally clients would come and confer with him there in the yard, but it was too hot to go back to the office.

He realized the importance of travel and he loved to travel. He tried to make a trip each year. Grandmother did not like to travel and really didn't want to go with him on any of these trips. He decided that the West was obviously going to be a growing place and he took a train trip to the West two or three times, and ended up in Oklahoma, before Oklahoma became a state. He bought a section of land there, I believe some six hundred acres at the outskirts of a very, very small town called Tulsa, Oklahoma. He kept this a couple of years and I think Oklahoma did become a state during that time, but he decided that Tulsa was not going to grow and he went back to Oklahoma, sold his land in Tulsa and bought a section of land in a town called Red Bird, Oklahoma. Unfortunately, Red Bird didn't thrive and Tulsa did, and at his death in 1947 the estate disposed of the land in Oklahoma.

He also disliked cold weather and so early on he would go to Florida in the winter. He bought a lot and built a house in Miami, Florida. For twenty-five years after that, every year the day after Christmas he and grandmother got in the Buick automobile and drove to Miami. It took two days to do that. They stayed until the first week in March. The annual meeting of the Sevier County Bank was held then and he returned for that.

He had become successful in the practice of law. He accumulated a lot of real estate, both residential and commercial, as well as farms. It worked out real well because when my father came into the family, he was a real estate dealer and he and my grandfather, under the name of Paine and Waters, bought a lot of land. Dad would find the land and Papaw would finance it, and they had a very successful partnership, and I'm very happy today that a lot of that land and property is still in the family. Our daughter, Cyndy Waters, lives in a house that her great-grandfather Paine bought up on Park

Road. When he died, my mother inherited it. When my mother died, I inherited it, and we renovated it a few years ago and it now belongs to Cyndy.

My sister Mary Louise graduated from the University in 1942 and went to Washington, D.C. to work. That was in the years of World War II. While she was in Washington she met R. B. (Pete) Hailey, who had graduated from the Naval Academy and served in submarines during World War II. In 1945 he had returned from the war and they decided to get married in Washington, D.C. They were married in the New York Avenue Presbyterian Church with Dr. Peter Marshall performing the wedding ceremony.

It was decided that we would all go up for the wedding. My brother David was in the Army then and unable to come home. Mother went up early to Washington to help make arrangements for the wedding. The plan was that Grandmother and Papaw and my father and I would come to Washington on the Tennessean. The Tennessean was a railroad train that left Memphis, came to Knoxville, departed Knoxville at 7 in the morning and arrived in Washington's Union Station at 7 o'clock that night. In other words, it took twelve hours to make the trip from Knoxville to Washington D.C. It was a very fine train and it was an exciting experience for me as a young fifteen-year-old boy. The plan was that on the day of our trip, early that morning we would go up to Grandmother's house and have breakfast and would leave there, go into Knoxville and catch the Tennessean, which means we had to get up very early.

Dad got up and went somewhere to do some business and I got up and went up to the house. Papaw was lying on the couch fully dressed and he said, "Johnny, where's John?"

And I said, "Well, he's off somewhere, Papaw. He'll be up here directly."

"Well," he said, "Susie's running around the house somewhere with her slip on." Grandmother didn't want to get her dress dirty so she was cooking breakfast for us, dressed in her slip. "I told Susie," Papaw said, "Susie, by God, put your dress on."

"Now, Papa, we're going to Mary Louise's wedding and going to leave the cussin' at home," Grandmother said.

"Well," he says, "I'm going to have a hell of a lot to catch up on when I get home."

We got to Knoxville on time and caught the Tennessean and went to

Washington. I well remember it because it was quite an experience for me, my first occasion of eating in the dining car of a train with all the linen and silver, which I thought was a very, very fine way to travel. When we arrived in Washington, we went to the Fairfax Hotel on Massachusetts Avenue. It's now the Ritz Carlton, home of the rather famous Jockey Club Restaurant that is still in that hotel to this day.

None of us had any thought of going to our rooms until we got Grandmother and Papaw settled in theirs, so we went with them with a bellman up to the room. He opened the door and there was the bedroom with twin beds. Papaw didn't like this and he asked the bellman, he says, "Boy, don't you have a room in this hotel for a man and his wife? I'm married to this woman and I want a room with a double bed."

Well, this bellhop was not about to deal with that. So he immediately called the manager and the manager came up and Papaw went through the same request with him. At that time hotels were very short and there simply wasn't any room, so Grandmother said, "Papa, we'll scoot the beds over real close and I can reach over and feel and see if you're all right."

Well, he didn't like that a bit but he had to settle for it.

At this time President Roosevelt had died and Truman was President of the United States and the vice-presidency was vacant. This was before the Constitution was changed to provide for selection of a vice-president when the office became vacant. Under the law at that time the president pro tem of the Senate held the office of vice president. Senator Kenneth D. McKellar from Tennessee was president pro tem of the U.S. Senate and had the office of vice president. My grandfather was a Democrat and he had in times past been a supporter of Senator McKellar. Senator McKellar sent the vice president's car over for my grandfather to use, and put it at his disposal during that time. But my grandfather was mad at McKellar for some political reason and wouldn't ride in the car, which I thought was a terrible waste. I tried my best to talk him into using the car because I thought that would have been really something. But he refused. Senator McKellar did come to the wedding, however.

The wedding came off as planned and was a very, very nice wedding and we all returned home, again on the Tennessean. Not too long afterward, my grandfather's health began to fail. This was his last trip and he died two years later.

JBW U.S. Navy picture

USS Conway 507 at Golfe Juan France December 1953
Mediterranean Moor stern to dock - anchor out

MY NAVY DAYS, 1952-1955

As a boy I admired the Navy. I suppose my love of the river and boats led me to prefer the Navy. The first naval officer I remember seeing was Alger Bowers. He was the brother of Gordon Bowers, our next door neighbor, and he came to visit occasionally. We called him "Mr. Alger." When I was a very young boy, I remember seeing him in the back yard of the Bowers home in his white uniform playing with a golf ball and a putter. I thought him to be a very important person. Mr. Alger graduated from the Naval Academy at Annapolis. Many years later when I was an ensign, Patsy and I visited Admiral and Mrs. Bowers at the Armed Forces Staff College in Norfolk, where he was the commanding officer.

When I went to the University of Tennessee in 1947, ROTC was required. UT had only Army and Air Force ROTC, no Navy. I joined the Naval Reserve in 1948 and attended drills at the Naval Armory on Alcoa Highway. At the end of my sophomore year I went on a two-week cruise to Veracruz, Mexico as part of my Naval Reserve training. After graduation in 1952 I entered the Naval Officers Candidate School in Newport, Rhode Island on September 1. I graduated and was commissioned on December 22, 1952.

In January of 1953 I reported for duty at Norfolk, Virginia to the ship USS Conway DDE 507, a destroyer. The Conway was commissioned on August 19, 1942. This was the second ship of the fleet to bear the name of William Conway, Quartermaster, U. S. Navy, who, while on duty in Pensacola Navy Yard on January 12, 1861, was ordered to haul down the American flag in token of surrender to Confederate forces. Conway promptly and indignantly refused. It was for this heroism that the ship bears the name. She served well in World War II. On November 8, 1950 she was commissioned again after having been converted to an escort destroyer. She was overhauled in the Norfolk Naval Shipyard in June, 1952. On September 16, 1953 she departed for a cruise overseas to the Mediterranean, and no hostilities were anticipated.

The Conway had left Norfolk two days before I reported. The ship had gone to Guantanamo Bay, Cuba for refresher training. I met Bob Weaver, who had graduated in my class at OCS, who was also reporting to the Conway. We lived a few days in the Bachelor Officers Quarters, BOQ, before boarding the USS Aldebaran, named after a star. The Aldebaran was a refrigerator supply ship going to Cuba. This was the second time I had been to sea. I learned the difference between a supply ship and a warship. Life was easy on the Aldebaran. We ate very good meals taken from the refrigerated storage, and The ship's one five-inch gun had not been fired in many years.

The Navy base at Guantanamo Bay, Cuba was organized to provide refresher training for Navy ships. Each ship in the Atlantic fleet was required to go there every two years for intensive training. Each day a group of observers would come on board early in the morning. The ship got under way, and the training exercises commenced. Gunnery exercises consisted of firing at target sleds and at sleeves pulled by aircraft. Shore bombardment was conducted on Calibra Island, an uninhabited island. Tons and tons of projectiles have been fired on this island for many years. Damage control and engineering drills were also conducted. Anti-submarine exercises were run with submarines which were also in the training. It was very exhausting. The observers were very strict, and the grades assigned were important. The Conway did not do very well and received an unsatisfactory grade on some exercises. An night we anchored in the harbor and frogmen attempted to get aboard and break our security. The battleship Iowa was at Guantanamo, and we heard that a frogman had slipped aboard and locked the captain in his stateroom. We doubled our guard. We worked very hard. It was hot even though it was January. We were all worn out when we finally got to our bunks each night.

Our captain was Commander J. D. Reese. He was very strict. I learned a lot at Gitmo, as we called it, but I wondered what I had gotten into.

I had not been on board many days when the captain, at the evening meal, asked who was the junior officer of the deck on the 4 to 8 a.m. watch. I told the captain I was JOD on the 4 to 8. He told me to have the messenger walk the main deck at sunrise and collect any flying fish that had flown aboard during the night for his breakfast. I decided that I would not fall for this trick and immediately forgot the order. I was very embarrassed when, the next morning, he asked for the flying fish. I learned that especially in the Caribbean it is not unusual for flying fish to hit the deck and not be able to get back into the water.

It was decided that I would be a division officer in charge of about forty deck hands who chipped, painted, and otherwise kept the outside of the ship in good shape. There were two deck divisions. My boss would be the first lieutenant who was in charge of the deck on warships. The chief boatswain mate was in our division. I was told that I would be in training for first lieutenant.

As a junior officer I stood an Officer of the Deck (OD) watch in port and a Junior Officer of the Deck (JOD) at sea. An officer's reputation on a destroyer is based on how he handles the ship. We were in maneuvers with many other ships a lot of the time. Changing course, speed, and formations are difficult to learn and can be very dangerous, especially at night and in bad weather. Captain Reese was a good ship handler. I tried to learn from him

At night when new maneuvers or formations were ordered, the captain would be called from his sea cabin. He would come on deck and almost immediately could comprehend the situation. He would then say, "I have the Conn," take charge, and maneuver the ship to its new station. The Combat Information Center (CIC) made maneuvering board solutions with radar and other plotting aids, but a good conning officer was generally ahead of "combat" as we called them in the intercom.

My goal was to be a good officer of the deck and I worked hard to qualify. Very soon after I got on board, we got a new executive officer, Lt. A. M. Brouner. Brouner was probably the best naval officer I knew in the Navy. I became his student. In September we left for the Mediterranean Sea to join the Sixth Fleet for five months. Before we left, we lost by transfer a number of our more experienced officers. We were short of ODs.

The captain ordered Brouner to take three junior officers and qualify them as officers of the deck as soon as possible. I was one of the three selected. In a short time the captain qualified all three of us and I began to stand a top watch.

I have said that Captain Reese was a good ship handler. One incident caused him considerable trouble. However, he got out of it with no damage to his career.

We had been to sea for several days and were scheduled to go into Little Creek, just south of Norfolk, and anchor one evening. We were to engage in amphibious exercises early the next day.

I had the deck (OD) and Brouner was the navigator. He selected an anchorage and marked it on the chart. I was proceeding to the place designated to anchor. It was about six p.m. There were a lot of ships in the harbor and I was being very careful and going slow. Captain Reese came on the bridge and asked me what I was doing. I told him that I was going to the anchorage, and that it was a little over a mile away. He turned and went back into his sea cabin, but almost immediately returned to the bridge and asked me, "Why don't we anchor here?" I replied that the navigator had selected the place to anchor and I was going there. He was irritated and said, "I have the Conn. Drop the hook." The chief ordered the seamen standing by with a sledge hammer to knock out the pin, and the big anchor clamored into the sea. The captain ordered "all back to stop the ship," and the Conway swung on the anchor. About nine o'clock (2100 hours military time) the Coast Guard harbor patrol signaled us that we were in a restricted area and over a harbor defense cable.

The captain ordered me to take charge of the anchor detail. I ordered the chief to "bring her up very slowly." When the anchor cleared the water, we saw shining, silver-looking cables running over the anchor. They were very tight, and we had to hook grapnel hooks to get them loose. We were ordered into port for an investigation. We later learned we had done several million dollars in damages. The Exec and I were very worried that we would likely be required to testify, and the captain would look very bad. Captain Reese left the ship and returned in a few hours. He announced that the investigation was over. He said that he pointed out that the chart was poorly marked and could not be easily seen on the bridge.

On September 16, 1953, the Conway left Hampton Roads, Virginia and sailed into the Atlantic Ocean, commencing a five-month tour of overseas duty. We were to be part of "NATO Operation Mariner", an operation that carried the Conway just seven miles short of the Arctic Circle in an area of high, turbulent seas and strong winds. The ship was pitched about as though it was just a plaything for the elements. The Conway participated in eighteen days and nights of complicated exercises with as many as thirty other ships. We had operations with the commander of the Sixth Fleet who was on the Des Moines, a cruiser. I will never forget that his radio call was "Jehovah," which I thought was appropriate. After these exercises ended, we proceeded to our first overseas port, Palermo, Sicily, arriving on October 9, 1953. Commander D. L. Byrd relieved Commander Reese during this tour. The ship returned to Norfolk on February 8, 1954.

The officers during the cruise were Cdr. Byrd, Cdr. Reese, Lt. Brouner, Lt. Sauer, LtJGs Trotti, Rosback, Strawmire, Olson, Cavallara, Craig, Mayzell, Cordes, Maak, and Hollander, and Ensigns Waters, Weaver, Wright, Ost, Burt, Ericson, Blackmore, St. Martin, and Dubois.

The ship visited the ports of Palermo, Caglairi, Istanbul, Suda Bay, Athens, La Apezia, Toulon, Toranto, Naples, Golfe Juan, Leghorn, Alicante, Gibraltar, and the Azores.

It was very interesting to be in the "Med," and this was my first time to be away from home during the Christmas holidays.

When we returned to Connus (Navy for Continental United States), LtJG Stawmire, the gunnery officer, was scheduled to get out of the Navy soon. LtJG Jack Cremmis was scheduled to become Gun Boss, and I would be his first lieutenant. Jack Cremmins had lost of number of foul weather jackets for which he had signed. Captain Reese was really after him because he could not account for the jackets.

We walked up the head of the pier to a pay phone booth and Jack called his U.S. senator from Massachusetts. The senator was John Kennedy and Jack knew him well. In fact, Cremmins' father worked for the Kennedy family. Cremmins told Kennedy he wanted a transfer off the Conway. The very next day Cremmins received a dispatch order transferring him to Boston, Massachusetts to be the recreational officer at the Naval District Headquarters in Boston. (Patsy and I visited him at his "recreational post" when I was attending Gunnery School in Newport).

The captain called me into his stateroom and told me I would be the new head of the Gunnery Department. To be Gun Boss you had to go to Gunnery School in Newport, Rhode Island. Of course, I had never been to Gunnery

School, but I was immediately ordered to go. Patsy and I left for Newport. We enjoyed being in Newport even though I did not learn a lot about Navy gunnery.

I knew that I was poorly prepared to be the gunnery officer. More than one hundred men would be under me, including all deck personnel, boatswain mates, gunners' mates, torpedomen, fire controlmen and sonarmen.

The Conway had a five-inch gun forward and aft. Two three-inch 50 twin mounts were on the 01 Deck (one deck above the main deck). The five-inch guns were controlled by a gun director located over the bridge. Down in the lower decks was the plotting room with the Mark 1A computer. This mechanical computer was about the size of a refrigerator lying on its side, and it took four men to operate. I can only guess what kind of modern equipment does that job today. The three-inch 50 battery had a more modern system. Since we were an anti-submarine ship, we had the latest sonar equipment with the 102 fire control system. Our depth charge battery was old and in very poor shape.

The ship had done very poorly in gunnery exercises. The five-inch guns worked fairly well, but the three-inch 50, torpedos and K guns were generally out of commission.

The previous gunnery officer did not use the chiefs and never asked them to do anything. They stayed in the chiefs' quarters and played cards.

When I returned from Gunnery School, I was made head of the gunnery department. I had four officers and four chiefs under me. None of the officers had any gunnery experience. Bob Weaver had been to Sonar School and was sonar officer. He was doing a good job and I left him alone.

I had the chief gunner's mate, the chief torpedoman and the first class fire controlman come to my stateroom. I told them I intended to run the department much differently. I knew very little naval gunnery, but I knew the department was in bad shape. I knew they were not up to date on the situation. I told them I wanted them to take a week and then tell me the condition of the department and what it was going to take to get it fixed. I told them I was not going to tell them what to do or manage their work, but, when the Conway had its next gunnery exercises, I expected the guns to fire. I knew the exercise was more than a month away.

I reminded them of the fire procedure, which they knew very well. When the ship was entering the firing exercise, the captain would receive permission to fire from the OTC (the Officer in Tactical Command). The captain would make sure the ship was in position, with safety bearings and so on. He would then inform me at Gun Control, "Mr. Waters, you may fire when ready." At this point, I told the chiefs that I would immediately order, "Commence fire." My predecessor used to take several minutes to check everything several times before he would order to fire. I asked each chief if he could handle his post. I told them I did not want an answer that day, but I would expect an answer within the next week.

The next day was a sight to see. All guns were being dismantled and spare parts were being brought on board. The captain wanted to know what was going on. I asked him to please bear with us and promised we would clean up the mess and restore order as soon as possible. Actually, I did not have any idea how long it would take.

To me the firing exercise was nothing short of a miracle. Everything worked perfectly. Every gun fired and fired well. Our target hits were only fair, but better than the ship had done since any one on board could remember.

I had been particularly worried about our depth charge battery. The K guns threw a depth charge about a hundred feet off to the side of the ship. On the stern, depth charges were rolled off racks. It took eleven depth charges to make a full pattern to cover a good sized area designed to hit the submarine. It was easy to roll the charges off the stern, but the Conway had not fired a full pattern in four years. The K guns were old and had taken a beating from salt water which came over the side.

The chief torpedoman was in charge of the depth charges. He was a small man and very quiet. I felt he hit the bottle a lot. When I was told we were to fire a full pattern, I was really worried. I had never seen a K gun fire or a depth charge explode. The chief torpedoman was not encouraging. He wanted me to try to get out of the exercise. I told him that we had to fire.

As I recall, there were four ships in the depth charge exercises. Each ship moved into position and, on orders from the squadron commander who was always called Commodore, fired its full pattern. Some of the ships got off a few K guns and there were three or four depth charge explosions. The depth charges were to be set to go off at 150 feet depth. It was going very badly. The Conway was to be the last ship to fire. I had the chief torpedoman with me at Gun Control, which was located on an open deck just aft of the pilothouse. The captain could come out of the pilothouse and talk to me face to face. I had a very low feeling about this exercise. I asked the chief, who I suspected had already had a few drinks, "Are we going to look bad? Will any of our K guns fire?" He said, "All K guns will fire." About that time the captain came out of the pilothouse and asked, "My God, John, can we fire?" It was too late to be uncertain or express doubt, so I replied, "Captain, the Conway will fire all eleven!" His expression indicated that he wondered if I had any idea what I was talking about.

The Conway was ordered into position. We commenced our run to go over the target, the location of the make-believe submarine. "Combat" was given range and bearings to the target. I ordered "Fire." The chief closed the firing key. It was a beautiful sight to behold. Every K gun fired on the exact time. The stern charges rolled off as planned and in perfect order. Eleven depth charges exploded, sending towering gushes of water high in the air. The Commodore gave up a "Well done!" All of a sudden I was considered a good Gun Boss.

Later that day I went down to the chiefs' quarters to congratulate the chief torpedoman. He was sitting at a table drinking coffee. After I had told him how much I appreciated his work, he said, "Mr. Waters, I know you really didn't think we could fire a full pattern, but I want to tell you I have never failed to do so since I have been a first class or chief." I said, "Chief, that is wonderful. You might have told me that before today."

We fired many gunnery and ASW exercises. On some we did very well and on others not so well. We never failed to fire. That is, I never had a gun out of commission when we were scheduled to fire.

Another event sticks in my mind. It caused me to acquire a nickname for a short time.

The Conway was in exercises with a large number of destroyers and the Battleship Iowa. A drone shoot was scheduled. The drone was a small, unmanned airplane. The wing span was about six feet. The drone was remote-controlled from the battleship. The drone would make runs from forward to aft alongside both ships. You were allowed to shoot for only a few degrees. It was almost impossible to hit the drone as it was small and very maneuverable. The object was to try to get proximity bursts (if the projectile got within thirty feet of the drone, it would burst). We fired non-fragmental projectiles so as not to destroy the drone. We were firing the three-inch 50 battery. When the gun ceased firing, there was a light on the control which indicated whether the gun was empty or if there was a round still in the chamber. This light was called the Bore Clear Light. It was very important to have the gun empty. If a round was still in a hot gun, you could have a "cook-off." That meant the gun would fire.

The Conway did all right in the shoot, and we were ordered to cease fire and report if all bores were clear. The gun captain noticed that Bore Clear Light was on and reported to me, "All bores clear." I so reported to the captain. We moved out to the left and started to overtake the battleship and return to the screen. The three-inch 50 starboard gun, when secured, pointed directly off the starboard side. About the time we got alongside the battleship, the gun captain reported to me that we had a loaded gun. The Bore Clear Light had malfunctioned! Here I was with the gun pointed directly at the battleship, and it would take several minutes for us to pass. I certainly did not want the gun to fire into the Iowa. I wanted to return to the screen and safely unload the gun. However, I was afraid of a "cook-off." I ordered the gun captain to elevate the gun to 90 degrees. In other words, stick it straight up in the air. I hoped no one would notice. Unfortunately, the battleship did notice and asked us why the gun was in that position. We had to "fess up." The battleship ordered us to proceed to a safe place ten miles away and unload through the muzzle (fire off the round). This was very embarrassing for me. That night I overheard some of the men talking. One said, "Bore Clear Waters had a bad day!"

On the Conway's second trip to the Mediterranean, Commander D. L. Byrd was on board. In a very short time we also lost A. M. Brouner as executive officer. Captain Byrd was a fine man and a very fine officer.

I was very proud to serve in the U.S. Navy. I learned a lot. I learned that the big majority of men will respond well to respect and courtesy and I learned how to work with people who were under me, but who knew a lot more about the work than I did. These lessons have served me well throughout my life.

JBW speaking at Sevierville Courthouse

Left to right: George Ed Wilson, Jimmie Quillen, JBW, Erby Jenkins, Frank Qualles, Howard Baker, Sr., Bill Brock, about 1963.

President Gerald Ford, Lamar Alexander, and JBW

Patsy and JBW preparing to go to the inauguration
of Richard Nixon in 1968.

POLITICS

As a boy I followed my father around Tennessee and especially East Tennessee. He was interested in politics and was involved in many campaigns. I suppose by doing this I picked up my interest in politics.

When I went to the University of Tennessee one of the first people I met was Howard Baker. Howard had been discharged from the Navy and was a law student. Our families had been acquainted and my uncle Cap Paine was a very close friend of both Howard and Irene Baker, Howard's father and stepmother.

Student politics were taking on more importance at UT. World War II was over and a lot of veterans had returned to the university. The fraternities had all been reactivated after the war. Both Howard and I were in the minority group of formerly small fraternities which were, in the student elections that year, challenging the old established fraternities that were known at the Big Ten. A new student political organization was formed and a very active campaign was conducted with Howard Baker being elected president of the student body.

Several years later, after I had graduated from the university, gone in the Navy, got out and graduated from law school, I was elected to the Republican State Executive Committee. I had always felt that the state party had been delinquent in not electing Republicans to state offices during the Eisenhower years. Eisenhower had carried Tennessee. The neighboring state of Kentucky had elected statewide senators and governors and I thought we should have done better.

Howard's father, Congressman Baker, had died in 1964 and his stepmother, Mrs. Irene Baker, was elected to succeed him for the unexpired term. Many people thought Howard should seek election to his father's seat after Mrs. Baker fulfilled the unexpired term but Howard simply was not interested in doing this. He had a high regard for his father's performance and ability, but Howard's technique was quite different from that of Mr. Baker. Congressman Baker gave great attention to detail. He dogged a problem or job until it was solved or finished. The senator works differently. He will give any problem a priority rating and he will also create a deadline date for decision or involvement. He delegates detail, but wants to ensure he has the best pro and con facts. Senator Estes Kefauver had died in 1961 and Mr. Hub Walters from Morristown had been appointed by Governor Clement to fulfill the term until the next election. So, in 1964, the remaining two year portion of Senator Kefauver's unexpired term was up for election. Senator Albert Gore, Sr. was also up for election in 1964 so we had a rather unusual situation with two United States senators up for election at the same time. The terms are staggered and they generally don't come up at the same time unless a death or resignation occurs. Dan Kirkendall of Memphis had already announced for the Republican nomination for the Gore seat. I felt very strongly that we should run a good Republican candidate for the balance of Kefauver's term and that this candidate should definitely be from East Tennessee. This would give us the opportunity to have a strong candidate from West Tennessee (Dan Kirkendall) as well as a good Republican candidate from East Tennessee. It was obvious that the Democrats were going to have a difficult time with a hard primary because Governor Frank Clement was a candidate and Representative Ross Bass was opposing him in the Democratic primary.

Howard and I had not kept in close contact during the years since college. I had worked quite a bit with Congressman Baker, his father, on some state party matters since I had been on the state committee. I had always delighted in my acquaintance with Congressman Baker and indeed his wife, Irene, who was a native of Sevier County. I have never known a more genuine gentleman. I don't believe any man ever served in the Congress who had a more personal concern for his constituents than did Howard Baker, Sr.

Some time in the early part of 1964 I called Howard on the phone and asked to come and see him in his office in Knoxville. Howard told me he would be delighted to oppose Ross Bass but he thought Frank Clement would be much more difficult. Like all of us at that time, he expected Clement to win the Democratic nomination.

An interesting side note is that later on at the height of the campaign Howard told me that he thought Ross Bass was going to beat Frank Clement. I couldn't see it and I believe that Howard was one of the few people in the state who predicted the Bass victory in the 1964 Democratic primary.

At our first meeting Howard refused to make a commitment about whether he was interested in running, but he promised me that he would consider the race and said he wanted to talk to his family about it. He asked me to return to his Knoxville office the following week.

At our second meeting he agreed to make the race if I would be his state campaign manager. I remember my reply was, "Until that moment I had thought you could wage a first class campaign, but if I was the best you could do for a campaign manager it was indeed going to be a tough campaign." We found out that I was right.

My first concern about the state manager's job was that I knew Howard needed the active support of the Knoxville Journal, which was the strong Republican daily newspaper in the state. The editor, Guy Smith, and I had not been political friends since I had made a race against B. Carroll Reese, the late Republican congressman from the first district. Of course, I lost that race. Much to my surprise, Howard said that he had discussed this with Mr. Smith and Smith had agreed. This was indeed an instance worthy of note since Smith was not well known for forgiving political enemies.

After our second meeting in Howard's office, we left his office and went down to the Farragut Hotel coffee shop for coffee. At that time it was a popular hangout for lawyers and politicians. They would come in mid-morning or mid-afternoon for a break and a cup of coffee. As we entered the coffee shop a group of lawyers were seated at a table, some of whom I knew and some I did not know. Howard asked me if I knew George W. Morton, a Knoxville attorney who was with the group. I knew him only by reputation as an outstanding lawyer. Howard wanted George in the campaign and we asked him to join us. After George recovered from the shock, I was happy that we now had a candidate, two supporters and the promise of help from a daily newspaper.

As a member of the Republican State Committee, I felt as if I had an opportunity to get a good start for the Baker campaign, so I invited the committee to meet in Gatlinburg, Tennessee. The committee had never met, in recent years at least, anywhere but Nashville, but they agreed to meet in Gatlinburg on April 4, 1964. State Representative Fred Atchley, who represented Sevier County in the state house at that time, and I had decided to have a joint gathering of both Republican members of the state House and Senate and the Republican State Committee. We arranged a dinner meeting at the Gatlinburg Inn and planned a program which was open to all Republicans. Republicans across the state were invited. I felt like this was a good opportunity to get some reaction to a Baker campaign. I sent out qualifying petitions to committee members and other Republicans I knew, to qualify Howard for the Senate race. In the press coverage for the Gatlinburg meeting I leaked to the press that qualifying petitions for Baker were being circulated in all congressional districts in the State of Tennessee. Howard and his wife Joy attended the Gatlinburg meeting and I was pleased that many Republicans encouraged him to make the race.

Harry Welford, a Memphis attorney, was a member of the state committee. He and Howard were acquainted and Welford was enthusiastic about the possibility of the race. Howard, Harry and I talked into the night at the Greystone Hotel, where Howard was staying. Suddenly we had a man in Memphis. The only problem was that there were a lot of cities, counties and people in between and we didn't have much there at that time. Harry later was appointed as a federal district judge and finally to the U.S. Court of Appeals.

The 1964 race was something new in Tennessee. In almost all of the ninety-five counties in Tennessee, we had no organization. We would go into a rural Middle or West Tennessee county, talk to any one we could, a lawyer, old school friend, or anyone we could find who would talk to us. Many times it was a Democratic office holder or leading citizen in that county. Many of these people would give us good advice. They would tell us whom we should see and what the local issues were in the town or county. One pleasant surprise was that the Democratic organization was old and much weaker than we thought. We put together what we could and moved on. When Howard came through to campaign in the Middle and West Tennessee counties we would sometimes be surprised to find that quite a bit of work had been done and a small crowd of enthusiastic supporters were working for us. Many times there was nothing in the way of an organization. Howard would ask, "What are we going to do here?" I would answer, "We're going to walk the streets."

Howard's best technique in campaigning was to have a few minutes with a voter. When he could talk to a person he left a very good impression. The voter remembered him and liked him. He did this well. He did not do the "handshake, hello, and move on" as well as Frank Clement or Estes Kefauver.

Howard ran an excellent race. We had an awful lot of good people who worked very hard for him and we came close to victory. But as the old politician said, "Close only counts in horseshoes." It doesn't count in winning elections.

After the 1964 defeat there was considerable discussion about future plans. "What are we going to do now?" I suppose all defeated candidates face this question. Of course, Ross Bass had the seat for the next two years. He had defeated Governor Clement in the primary and narrowly defeated Baker in November by two percent of the vote. We had a lot of advice from many sources. People were telling Howard what he ought to do. We met and Howard decided that it was impossible to make an intelligent decision on this matter until January of 1966. Bass had the seat for two years. The question was, how would he get along? Lyndon Johnson had won a landslide victory over Barry Goldwater for the presidency. He was considered very popular. Would Johnson be able to maintain his popularity? Would the Great Society succeed or would LBJ stub his toe? Would the Republican Party broaden its base nationally away from the Goldwater concept? Or was it dead? There were a lot of people who thought the party was dead.

Of course, what happened was history. Ross Bass was not as popular as we thought he might be. As a matter of fact, he was unable to really handle his Senate seat very well and made a number of people mad at him in Washington and in Tennessee. And Lyndon Johnson's popularity steadily declined as well.

But Howard had decided to wait until January, 1966 to see what happened. What did happen was that Ken Roberts of Nashville could not wait. He announced that he was going to run for the Senate seat and some of Baker's 1964 supporters jumped to the conclusion that Baker would not run. They wanted to support a candidate and Ken Roberts appeared to be an attractive candidate, so some went to Roberts. What happened was that we ended up with a 1966 primary against a strong opponent.

Ken Roberts was well financed, but Baker was successful and there was some surprise because this time Frank Clement beat Ross Bass so Bass was out and our opponent this time was Frank Clement. The campaign that fall was hard fought, but we had the nucleus of an excellent organization put together and we built on it quickly. The result was that Howard Baker was the first Republican to be popularly elected by the people of Tennessee to the United States Senate.

Howard opened his Washington office and his Tennessee field offices and immediately became a very popular United States senator. He was popular in Washington; he was popular with his colleagues, and of course he was very popular in Tennessee. It certainly didn't hurt Howard that his father-in-law, Everett Dirksen, was the minority leader of the Republicans in the United States Senate. Senator Dirksen was a colorful man and a man that it was my privilege to get to know. Dirksen stories will be told for many, many years about his conduct and how he ran the Senate. He had a great speaking voice and was a very bright man and a strong leader for the Republican Party during those years.

The next important event on the political scene was the 1968 convention to decide who would be the Republican nominee to run for president for the next term. Because of Vietnam, Johnson had become pretty unpopular and decided that he would not run, and the Democratic Party was generally in great disarray. Their national convention that year in Chicago was almost a catastrophe. Hubert Humphrey got the nomination, but it was a tough situation for the Democrats.

The 1968 Republican Convention was held in Miami in August. I was elected as a delegate from the First Congressional District. The district convention was held in Greeneville and Carl Young from Johnson City was the other delegate. Bob McInturff from Bristol and Ted Wellocks from Jefferson County were alternates.

Nixon was the favorite to get the nomination. Governor Ronald Reagan had the more conservative support and Governor Rockefeller from New York had the more liberal support. Rockefeller had trouble deciding whether he wanted to run or not and was in and out a number of times before he finally decided to seek the nomination. Almost all so-called experts gave Nixon a first ballot victory or a total within fifty votes of first ballot victory. However, it was generally believed that Nixon would have to win on either the first or second ballot. Many gave him only the first ballot and then it was generally expected that his strength would drop dramatically and someone else might have a chance. For this reason the delegates' second choice was widely discussed. Both Rockefeller and Reagan expected to come to the top and win after Nixon slipped. Tension developed among the delegates. After you did your duty and voted for Nixon on the first ballot, who would you vote for next? There was considerable worry in the party that the 1964 Goldwater race would be a real problem to overcome and votes for the conservative Reagan might give him the nomination. What struck fear in the Nixon camp was that everyone seemed to expect to have to make a second choice. In retrospect I think the delegates were merely preparing themselves. After all, after Nixon the choices were very far apart.

I decided that I would probably go for Rockefeller. The polls showed Rockefeller with the best chance to win and I absolutely felt for the good of the country that the Republicans must win. I believed 1964 to be a dark period in our party's history and I wanted no rerun of that event.

We all recognized that Ronald Reagan was an extremely attractive candidate. I well remember, when he visited the Tennessee delegation in Miami, how well he looked and how he conducted himself. I knew that he could be a very good candidate. I believe that the delegates were generally concerned about this decision: who to support if Nixon failed. Most of them were aware of the tremendous importance of this decision, if it ever had to be made. All of us had some doubt, and most respected our fellow delegates' opinions even if they conflicted with our own.

Nixon's first ballot nomination was somewhat of a relief to all.

Howard Baker became a truly great United States senator, perhaps one of the very small number of men and women who served in the Senate who truly built a remarkable record. His service as vice chairman of the Watergate inquiry brought him a lot of recognition, and then being elected minority leader for the Republican Party and later serving as majority leader of the United States Senate indicated how really powerful and how well liked he really was. I know that not only was Howard popular enough among his Republican colleagues to be elected their leader, but he had tremendous respect from the other party. A poll one time showed that he could have been selected as majority leader by vote of the Democratic members of the United States Senate.

I've always valued my friendship with Howard Baker very highly. He is a great man, a man of great compassion, intelligence, integrity and tremendous ability. I witnessed the sad time when his wife Joy died. I was very fond of Joy. We were close friends. But I'm happy to say now that he has married the former senator from Kansas, Nancy Kassebaum, and they are very happy and enjoying these happy years together. We are all very, very pleased.

Randy Sykes, JBW, R.B. (Pete) Hailey, Ron Sharp
Hailey, Waters, Sykes & Sharp

LAWYERING

Becoming a lawyer was very definitely one of my most prized accomplishments. I love the profession; I like lawyers. I consider the practice of law a noble and a great calling. I am distressed when a lawyer fails his client in devotion and integrity. This failure sometimes happens. But I am more often sustained and proud when I witness the very excellent and good services rendered by lawyers for their clients' needs and causes. The general public does not, and perhaps cannot, appreciate or understand that a lawyer is evaluated by his or her fellow lawyers in relation to the effort, brilliance, determination and energy with which he or she advocates clients' causes.

The results of these efforts, the success or failure, the business of winning or losing, are indeed important but secondary in the scale of importance to the fellow lawyers.

Lawyers are the biggest critics of the "System" and will only defend it when it is in peril. Recorded history of the nation proves this fact time and time again.

The practice of law to me is being in the arena of what's happening. It reflects the current affairs, the current problems, the current "goings on." It is the "Now" and it is mortal and human with all its imperfections. It recognizes love, hate, generosity and greed. In every age and time it has reflected the goals and ambitions of man and his desire to attain the admiration and respect of his fellow man.

With two good lawyers and a honorable and impartial judge, truth and justice will prevail more often than they will fail. Indeed it has been said that our system of justice, basically the jury system, is an imperfect system, but it is the best system man has designed and created in all the years of civilization.

Years ago I heard a story about a debate between a lawyer and a physician. The question was which profession had made the most important contribution to our county and its people. The doctor was claiming that there was no comparison of the benefits produced by the two professions. The medical profession had cured the sickness, disease and injuries of the people and made possible a healthy and strong people. The lawyer responded, "While your practitioners in medicine were bleeding George Washington, mine were writing the Constitution of the United States."

In 1961 I commenced the practice of law in Sevierville, associated with my brother-in-law, R. B. (Pete) Hailey, and Frank Miller. Our offices were over the Sevier County Bank Building, now the Overbay Building on Court Avenue. Every law office in town was located on the second floor of one of the downtown buildings. Judge George R. Sheppard of Newport held the Circuit Court and Judge Buford A. Townsend was our Chancellor.

Sevierville was a busy town in 1961 and a good place to practice law. Gatlinburg was a nationally known resort town and was attracting large numbers of tourists. Pigeon Forge was developing rapidly but had not acquired the tourist trade that it enjoys today. Court Avenue housed Sevier County Bank and the Bank of Sevierville was five doors up, south on Court Avenue where the Charlie Johnson law office is today. The First National Bank was located on the Parkway in Gatlinburg. The new banks, Citizens National Bank, Tennessee State Bank, and First Federal Savings and Loan Association, came later. Mountain National Bank is a new addition.

In 1961 there were a hundred and twenty-one cases filed in the Circuit Court of Sevier County and a hundred and fifty-nine cases filed in the Chancery Court. Multiply that by twenty for today. The Register of Deeds office in the Sevier County Courthouse recorded three-thousand one hundred thirteen documents in 1961. This included deeds, trust deeds, leases, corporate charger and so forth. When I began practice in 1961 there were thirteen lawyers active in practice. Other than the three in Hailey, Miller and Waters there were Philip and T. M. Wynn; Robert Ogle, Sr. and Robert Ogle, Jr.; W. Henry Ogle; George G. Allen; Hansell Proffitt; and John Earl Cooksey. Gatlinburg had Thad B. Smith and Clay James. Mr. James had moved to Gatlinburg from Knoxville and did a limited practice. We had a good bar in

Sevierville in 1961. I counted them all as my friends and I would do absolutely anything to help any one of them unless it was to the detriment of my client.

In the early days the Circuit Court had three terms each year, and Chancery Court had two terms. When the Circuit Court met, the judge and the district attorney general came to Sevierville by horse or hack or by train or automobile. Usually a number of lawyers travelled with the judge and the attorney general. The group usually stayed in Sevierville in the Snapp House, the Mitchell House, the Central Hotel or other room-and-board houses. The term of the court might last one week or several weeks depending on the docket. Since a large number of jurors was summonsed into town, and, of course, the litigants and witnesses were also present, a term of court was definitely the "Big Event" in town at that time. During most of the past years, Sevier County was with Cocke, Jefferson, Grainger, Hancock and Union. Many years ago other counties were also included in the district.

The circuit-riding lawyer no longer exists. The judge and attorney general must still travel to different towns in their circuit, but usually return to their home each night. The term of court is no longer the big event it once was. Many lawyers from adjacent towns still appear in court in Sevierville, and Sevier County lawyers still have clients which they represent in the courts of other counties. Lawyers still enjoy the contest of the trial and there still exists a spirit of fellowship, but most of us realize that we've lost some of the thrill and excitement that the old circuit rider knew.

I wish that I had made notes on the humorous events that happened to me and the other lawyers during my early years of practice. I regret that I did not keep a better record. Even though lawyers are very opinionated and stubborn, they can enjoy a joke better than anyone, especially on an adversary.

Some of the most humorous events that I have ever witnessed happened in the courtroom or in talking to clients and doing their legal work. Especially in Sevier County, lawyering has always been a very important job, and for that matter a good profession to have. Sevier County was known in the early days as "a fertile mother of litigation." When I started practicing law in Sevier County Judge Ray L. Reagan had not been county judge very long. He came on the bench in 1958. Judge Reagan was not a lawyer. In fact, he had very little college education. He was a self-educated man and he was conclusive proof that the main qualities needed to be a good judge are a good judicial temperament and a sense of fairness. Judge Reagan had these traits.

Before Reagan became county judge, the justice of the peace system was still in effect and was the method used to try minor cases. Any justice of the peace could try minor cases or bind criminals over the grand jury and, quite frankly, the system had gotten somewhat out of hand before Judge Reagan became the county judge. The process was not being handled very well and there was considerable criticism about the justice of the peace court. Judge Reagan decided that he was going to take on those duties and try those cases, even though he actually was not required to do so. The county judge is now called a county executive and he is basically the chief administrative officer of the county. But Judge Reagan thought it was his duty to try these cases and he did an outstanding job. He had this sense of fairness that served him very well, even when he was trying a fairly complex law suit.

I think this is illustrated by a case one time that I was not involved in but I heard Judge Reagan try. This case was called a paternity lawsuit. That's a lawsuit where a pregnant woman sues a man that she alleges is the father of her unborn child, asking for support of that child. She must prove that this man is indeed the father of the child. In this particular case the defendant who was accused of being the father brought in five other men who were sworn in and testified that they had had sexual relations with the plaintiff, the prospective mother, during the time. That meant they could have fathered the child. The net result was that there were six men who could have been the father and the defendant claimed that there was no way to tell which of the six was the father.

Generally, in past litigation, this was held to be substantial proof to prevent a judgment against the defendant and the case would be dismissed. However, Judge Reagan, after hearing the whole case, brought the five witnesses and the defendant back into the courtroom. He said, "Now, I've heard this proof and one of you is the father of this child by your own admission. I don't know which one it is and you don't either. Now, gentlemen, the truth is this woman is going to give birth to this child and she has to have $300 to pay for the medical costs of this birth. That's the general cost of this in the county now and there's no doubt about it. She needs $300. So what I am doing, gentlemen, is telling you that I want each of you to find $50 to pay to this woman and I'm going to dismiss the case."

Well, it was kind of surprising, but each one of the men stood up immediately, paid the $50 and walked out. The next day the judge was talking to me and he asked, "Johnny, what do you think about that verdict?"

"Well, Judge," I said, "it may be well unheard of in the history of paternity suits for a verdict to go down like that where a witness is ordered to pay for a judgment when he wasn't even sued, but there's no question about it — you did the right thing and I think it's good justice!"

And that's exactly the way that Judge Reagan looked at these situations.

The justice of the peace system had been abused, but yet, there were literally hundreds of funny cases that were tried before justices of the peace back when justices were trying those lawsuits. Some of these justices had very little education or legal training, and some of them turned out to be pretty good judges.

One man, Squire Sutton, tried an awful lot of cases up in the Walden's Creek area. T. M. Wynn, a lawyer in Sevier County, told me this story. He said he hadn't been practicing law very long when a plaintiff had sued T. M.'s client, the defendant, claiming that he was entitled to a money judgment against the defendant for some debt or other cause of action. So they went out to Walden's Creek to Squire Sutton's home and found Squire Sutton sitting in a chair out under a tree. The plaintiff put on his case and T. M. cross-examined and put on his defense and raised every legal or factual issue he could think of in defense of the defendant. But when the case was all over, T. M. said, Squire Sutton, who had been sitting there all through the trial thumbing through the pages of a Sears and Roebuck catalog, said, "Judgment for the plaintiff in this case and the defendant will pay him $22.50."

T. M. stood up to object to the judge's ruling and wanted to know a little more about why the judge was ruling that way. But the defendant kind of pulled him by the coattail and told him to sit down. When it was all over the client observed that when Squire Sutton was through with the proof, he looked down at the page in the catalog where Squire Sutton was and saw a page advertising a .22 rifle for sale for $22.50. The defendant said to T. M., "Hush up and sit down before he turns on over and gets to where those pianos are in that book!"

T. M. said he learned an important lesson right there about trying lawsuits before justices of the peace.

Judge George R. Sheppard from Cocke County was the circuit judge during the early years of my practice and I tried literally hundreds of cases before Judge Sheppard when he would come over here and hold court. He was a very smart man, but he didn't tolerate a lot of wasted time in lawsuits. He wanted to get through with them, and as a matter of fact, he could dispose of more lawsuits in a short time than any judge I've known. Sometimes this irritated the trial lawyers because they didn't feel as if they had enough time to properly present their case. Judge Sheppard could be pretty tough in making the lawyer move on.

He had a habit that was annoying. When the lawyer was examining or cross-examining a witness, if the lawyer paused to check his notes or confer with his client or somebody else at his table, Judge Sheppard would immediately say, "Call the next witness! Call the next witness!" And sometimes even if the lawyer just paused to catch his breath to think about the next question, the judge would say, "Call the next witness! Call the next witness!"

It was well known that Judge Sheppard loved to play golf and if you were trying a lawsuit in the early afternoon and it was a pretty, sunny day and he was looking out the windows of that old second story courthouse room, he would want to end as soon possible so he could go play golf and he would make you move on pretty fast.

T. M. was examining his witness and he said it was a fairly complex case and every time he would stop to even catch his breath, the judge would say, "Call the next witness! Call the next witness!"

So one time T. M. looked at his notes and the judge said, "Call the next witness!" T. M. got up and said, "May it please the court, I know that your honor would like to dispose of this matter in a hurry and that Your Honor wants to move on as quickly as possible. I can assure Your Honor that I feel exactly the same way. I too would like to get this case disposed of and move on to other things. It's a beautiful day and I'm sure that all of us would like to be somewhere else other than in this courtroom, but I must tell Your Honor that in all fairness to my client and his case, there's just one more question that I feel that I have to ask this witness before he is excused, and I assure Your Honor that I would not ask this question unless I felt it was just absolutely necessary for my case."

Well, T. M. went on and on in this vein and, after about two minutes,

Judge Sheppard, who was a very small man anyway, was sitting in about the last two inches of his seat. Finally he threw his hands up in the air and said, "For God's sake, Mr. Wynn, ask the question!"

I think, at least in that case, T. M. gave the judge a lesson about giving lawyers the chance to ask the questions they felt were necessary to the law suit.

Judge Sheppard had a practice of setting a number of cases for trial on the same day. It was very difficult for a lawyer to know which one was actually going to end up being tried and you had to prepare for many cases even when you knew only one or two would be tried. Of course, a lot of cases are settled on the courthouse steps, as they say, so that having them set for trial will move them along and get them settled without having to be tried at all. But at any rate, Judge Sheppard was pretty bad about setting sometimes five or six cases for trial on a day when you knew only one or maybe two at the most could be tried.

We, at this point in time, were doing some defense work, defending automobile accidents in association with the Jenkins and Jenkins firm in Knoxville. They represented some insurance companies in defense cases and sometimes we would be associated in the same case. There was an automobile accident case and Erby Jenkins, a very prominent lawyer in Knoxville, was going to try it. He had asked Pete Hailey, my law partner, to help him try the case. The day the case was set for trial, I was eating breakfast when Pete called me on the telephone and said, "Johnny, I've got to go to Nashville today on an important matter that I can't get out of, and Erby Jenkins is coming up here to try this defense case we've got, and, of course, Erby knows all about the case and he was going to try it anyway. I was really just going to help him select the jury. Could you go over there and help him select the jury in this case and help him try the case? You won't have any problem because he'll try the case, anyway."

So I said, "Okay," and I went to the office to get the file. About 8:30 that morning I was sitting at my desk. Court was to start in thirty minutes and I was going through the file trying to figure out what the case was about when in the office walked Ray Lee Jenkins, Erby's son. Ray Lee is now and has for many years been a very prominent criminal court judge in Knoxville, but at this point in time he was working with his daddy's law firm. He had been named after the senior member of that firm, a very famous trial lawyer, Ray

Jenkins.

So Ray Lee walked in the office and said, "Johnny, where's Pete?"

And I said, "He's not here. He's gone to Nashville."

"Well," he said, "Daddy sent me up here. Said he had something else he had to do and he sent me up to try this lawsuit. He said Pete knew all about it and all I'd have to do is just help him out. This lawsuit's supposed to be set for trial today."

"Ray Lee," I said, "you and I are in big trouble."

I told him what Pete had done to me and we grabbed up the file and went across the street and thought we'd get this thing continued. We sat there through two or three cases that were set that had either fallen through the cracks, been settled, or for some other reason were not going to be tried. Then Judge Sheppard called this case, and I got up and said, "Your Honor, we'd like to get this case continued. Mr. Hailey was going to try this case and he's been called out of town on a rather unforeseen problem that took him to Nashville."

Judge Sheppard looked down and said, "Well, Mr. Jenkins is in this case. He can try the lawsuit."

Ray Lee got up and told him his story, and the judge said, "Now, gentlemen, I'm sick and tired of some of these continuances. Both of you two are good lawyers and you can just try this lawsuit." He turned to the plaintiffs and said, "Call the first witness and let's get on with trying this lawsuit."

So here we were trying a lawsuit that we were not prepared for. There had been a number of depositions taken so one of us would cross-examine a witness while the other read the deposition and read the file and tried to prepare the case. Thank goodness there were two of us! It was a fairly simple case and we struggled through it, but the most surprising thing of all was that when the case was over with, the jury returned a verdict in our favor, in favor of the defendant. It was very unusual in any kind of an automobile accident case at that point in time to get a defendant's verdict. We were both absolutely shocked that we were able to get away with that and not end up in serious trouble, which we perhaps should have been.

During this time there were no public defenders, so lawyers were just appointed by the judge. He might have a list so he would rotate, or he might look up and see who was sitting in the courtroom and appoint that lawyer to try a case for an indigent defendant, that is somebody that didn't have enough money to employ a lawyer. The lawyer that was appointed had to do the best he could to try the lawsuit. Lawyers didn't look forward to these kinds of appointments because they took up your time and there was no money whatsoever paid for the defense lawyers. Later an act passed so that the legislature set up a pool of money for appointed lawyers. That was very unsatisfactory as well, and later a public defender's office was created and the indigent clients were handled much better. But, in fairness, most of the lawyers who were appointed to defend an indigent defendant did the best they could with it.

One day I was sitting in the courtroom and a larceny case against Jesse James Carr was called and the judge appointed me to defend him. I talked to him about the lawsuit. He was in jail and couldn't make bond to get out. He was accused of stealing gas out of a car on a used car lot. It was a pretty bad case since the officer who arrested him saw him siphon the gas out of the car on the car lot, carry it in a can to his own car parked on the curb, and drive away. We went over to try the case and the state prosecutor had only one witness there and that was the arresting officer. They had failed to bring in the man who owned the used car lot where this larceny had taken place. The state went ahead and put the police officer on the stand, and the police officer testified that he had been watching Jesse James for some time and had been particularly watching him that day. He said he was sitting hidden across the road from the used car lot and he saw Jesse James drive up, park his car, take a five-gallon can and a hose out of the back of his car, and go over and siphon this gas out of this car on this used car lot, put the can in his car and drive off. He let him get two or three blocks down the road before he stopped him and arrested him.

And with that the state rested.

At this point I got up and moved that the case be dismissed, saying the state hadn't proved the essentials of stealing because they didn't prove that Jesse James didn't have permission from the owner of the used car lot to get that gas. Well, the judge recognized that as a good defense and dismissed the case and Jesse James walked out very much surprised, as I was. He went back to the jail, however, and told other prisoners what a good lawyer I was. Every indigent defendant over there was calling the court, asking that I be appointed to defend him and it was all I could do to get out of appointments. Sometimes doing a good job doesn't turn out to be too good a thing for your work load!

Another appointed case was interesting but could have gotten me into some trouble and I was very relieved that it didn't. It started when the police up in Gatlinburg arrested a young man who was proven to be twenty-one years old, but he was retarded and he only looked as if he was fifteen or sixteen years old. He'd been born and raised back up in the mountains and he was not very bright and kind of stunted in his growth as well. He got in with some men over in Gatlinburg and they gave him some beer, and got him into some troubles that ended up in his being arrested and brought in for trial and put into the Sevier County Jail. Again, I was appointed to defend him.

I went over to talk to the lad and he obviously didn't understand exactly what he'd done and needed help, and so I got ahold of what was then the Tennessee Department of Welfare to see if they couldn't give this kid some training or help, medical and psychological. He didn't need to be sent to the penitentiary. He needed to get some help and I thought maybe I could get him out. At that point in time, Tennessee was not as equipped as it is now to handle those things and even though a couple of people came up from Knoxville to talk to him, time went on and nothing was done. I had gotten the case passed two or three times and still nothing was done.

Ray Noland was the sheriff at that time and Ray was, in my opinion, one of the finest sheriffs we ever had. One day when I was over at the jail, Ray took me aside and said, "John, when are you going to dispose of this case?"

I said, "Ray, I'm trying to get him some help from the welfare department. The boy needs some professional help. He doesn't need to be convicted."

"Well," he said, "that's right. But you're not doing any good with that."

"No, I'm not," I agreed. "I'm working at it but I'm not doing any good."

"Well," he said, "John, this boy's been around here long enough in the jail. I've tried to protect him, but he's here with these other criminals and he's been here too long."

"Well, Ray," I said, "I don't know what we can do about it."

"Well," he said, "I tell you what I'm going to do. I'm going to let him escape."

"Escape!"

"Yeah, I'm going to set him up with a trusty and tell this trusty to tell him that if he's smart and does what the trusty tells him, he can escape and go home. If I was to turn him lose, he'd be right back in trouble up in Gatlinburg, but if he escapes I'm going to send word to him that if he comes to town any more, I'm going to be after him. I think I can scare him enough he will stay at home and not get into any more trouble. If I just release him, it won't work."

"Ray," I said, "that sounds like a pretty good idea to me."

So Ray set this up and, sure enough, the boy escaped, got home back up in the mountains, and Ray sent the word to him and nobody ever saw or heard of him again. But next term of court, I'm sitting in court and Judge Sheppard calls the docket and this case. I hadn't thought about it still being on the docket, although I certainly should have, and I said, "Please, Your Honor, I wish you'd pass this case on this call. I've got some information I need to get."

He did and he recessed later and went back to the room in back of the courtroom where he and the lawyers always went when court recessed. I went back there and I said, "Judge, I've got to tell you what happened in that case you called. I'm a little bit worried about it. I guess I've done the wrong thing. I guess it probably wasn't legal, but I'm just going to tell you what happened."

So I told him. I was kind of scared because I was thinking that I might be getting myself in serious trouble over doing such a thing like this. Much to my relief the judge said, "Johnny, I wish you and Ray Noland would let a whole lot more of them do that over there."

We got away with it.

One of the types of cases that I disliked handling was divorce cases, even though during the first seven or eight years I tried an awful lot of them. I think most lawyers made an effort to reconcile people in divorces when they could, even though I don't think lawyers get credit for it. I know that during the time I handled divorce cases most lawyers really tried to see if there was some way to keep the people together. Sometimes it was possible and sometimes it wasn't. I for one have certainly recognized that there are a number of people in marriages where divorce is the only solution to a bad situation. But many times it's really a tragedy and very unfortunate.

One day when I was in my office, the secretary came in and told me that a lady was there who had called in for an appointment and wanted to see me about a divorce. This woman came in and sat down. She was obviously a woman past middle age, a stout, strong woman who lived on her farm with her husband. I knew where their place was. She very reluctantly and sorrowfully told me that she had to get a divorce. She didn't want to. She and her husband had worked together on their little farm and the children were grown and gone. She simply could not tolerate the situation any longer. It was too unbearable.

"What happened?" I asked.

"He hits me," she said. "He's beat me up over the years a number of times. Sometimes it's just a slap or two, but it's gotten worse and sometimes it's pretty bad. Last time I was at the kitchen sink after supper, washing dishes, and he was mad and picked up the skillet and hit me with it and hurt me very badly. I've known for some time that it was getting worse and I just couldn't tolerate this any more. I hate to do it. I hate to get a divorce, but I can't stand it any more."

Well, I looked at her. As I said, she was a woman past middle age but a very strong, large woman. "Have you ever offered to hit him back?" I asked.

"Oh, no," she said, "I've never done that."

"Well, you know, you look like you're a pretty strong woman. You say you've worked on the farm in the fields with him, and I think you might ought to think about that."

"What do you mean?" she asked.

I said, "Well, why don't you go home and you go out in the barn and get a piece of two by four or maybe a mattock handle or pick handle or something like that ... a pretty good sized board. You just take it there in the house and the next time he comes at you, let him have it. Now, you'll have to hit him pretty hard. Don't just swipe at him. You'll have to hit him pretty hard. But you might break him of that."

"Oh," she said, "I've never thought about that. It never occurred to me to offer to hit him back."

"Well," I said, "I can tell you don't want a divorce, but you can't tolerate things the way they are. Maybe you can straighten this out."

Well, the woman left the office and, of course, after she got gone, I thought, "My goodness, why in the world did I give that woman that advice? That's the worst thing I could have possibly told her. That old man will probably kill her, and I'll be in serious trouble. Why in the world did I do that?"

Well, it bothered me pretty bad and I talked to my partner, Pete Hailey. He too thought it was a dumb thing to do. I worried about it for two or three days, but not too long after that my secretary came in and told me the woman was back. I said, "Show her in!"

She walked in and sat down and said, "Well, I came in here to thank you for your advice."

"Oh," I asked, "what happened?"

"I did exactly what you said. I went home and I went out to the barn and we had an old mattock handle there that the mattock had come out of. It was a pretty strong piece of handle about three feet long. I picked it up and I just carried it in the house and just sat it up there in the corner next to the sink. Two or three days went by and he never did anything. But the other night I was at the kitchen sink there doing the dishes and he got up and started cussin' and fussin' again. He came at me there to the sink and I just picked up that mattock handle and I hit him as hard as I could. I knocked him to his knees. I addled him pretty bad. I thought, 'Well, I'm going to have to hit him again,' and I drawed back to hit him again, but he begged me not to. He begged me to please, not hit him any more, and I told him I wasn't putting up with this any more.

"He's out here in the waiting room," she said, "and he wants to talk to you."

So I buzzed the secretary to bring him in and here comes in this little fellow, about half as big as the woman — a little, dried-up fellow. He sat down and he said, "I want to tell you, I want to promise to you, that I swear to God that I won't ever hit her again as long as I live. I don't want a divorce and I don't want her leaving. We're going to get along. And I just want to tell you ... she made me come in here and tell you. I swear I'll never do that any more."

Well, they left and that was the last that I ever heard of them. But I was awfully glad to get rid of that one. It was really awfully poor advice for a lawyer to give a client ... even though it did work.

One other divorce case had an interesting twist. This was the first client I ever interviewed as a lawyer. As a matter of fact, the incident happened when I was still a student at the University of Tennessee Law School, taking a course in Legal Clinic. A legal clinic set up in the UT Law School allows indigent people to come in and get advice from student lawyers under the supervision of a licensed practicing lawyer. It gives students experience in actual case matters. At the time I was a student there an awful lot of these cases that came into the clinic were divorce cases. The clients came in and had to fill out an affidavit and prove that they were indigent and unable to afford to get a lawyer before they could qualify to be helped at the clinic.

But the very first case that I was involved in, I was sitting in the little office in the basement of the school and they said this woman had come into the clinic and properly qualified and needed a divorce. They brought her in and sat her down in front of me. I was a little surprised, because she looked a little more prosperous than most of the clients we had at the clinic. She was fairly young, pretty well dressed and really an attractive woman. I was a little surprised because she certainly did not fit the type that we usually got in the clinic.

I asked her what the problem was and she said that she had to get a divorce from her husband. The situation was intolerable and she just couldn't stand it any more. We student lawyers kept a code in front of us to see what the allegation was that would account for a divorce. At that time the easiest grounds for divorce was called Cruel and Inhuman Treatment, but you still had to offer evidence that could be substantiated under the "cruel and inhuman treatment" law. It was not nearly as easy to do that as it is today under the law. But at any rate, during that interview she was telling me all these troubles, but she didn't come up with anything that was specific and I finally said, "Well, you're going to have to tell me exactly what it is that your husband does."

She looked at me and she said, "Well, he's got a hot finger."

Well, this really took me aback because I didn't know what she was talking about. I hesitated to ask a lot more questions, although I wondered what she meant. All kinds of things were running through my mind, and I finally decided I would just have to make her be more specific.

"Well," I said, "I'm not familiar with that. You're going to have to tell me what it is that he does and why you don't like it."

She said, "He's got a hot finger. He writes bad checks and I'm sick and tired of paying for them. He's in trouble with the law."

Well, I breathed a sigh of relief, because I'd never heard that expression before, describing someone who wrote bad checks. As a matter of fact, I've never heard it since!

One of Sevier County's colorful public officials was the late Bat Gibson. Bat served as sheriff of Sevier County during the early seventies. He had been a barber in Sevierville for years and was quite a colorful guy. He carried a huge pistol, a .357 magnum. At the time Bat was sheriff the popular television show, Dukes of Hazard, was on the air. The show involved law enforcement officers in a small Southern town. The main emphasis of the show was a lot of high-speed pursuit chases in automobiles, where the automobiles were often involved in wrecks. As a matter of fact, Bat wrecked more county cruisers that anybody, because he and some of his deputies tried to duplicate some of the stunts in the television show. But, at any rate, Bat was a piece of work.

I remember one day I was walking through the Sevier County Courthouse and somebody stopped me in the hall. "You ought to go in there and listen to this lawsuit they're trying in front of Judge Reagan. It's really funny!"

So I walked in the courtroom where Judge Reagan was trying this lawsuit. Bat had arrested the man who was sitting there at the counsel table. He was probably one of the first honest-to-goodness hippies who ever came through Sevier County. Up until that time we'd read about them in newspapers and seen them on television, but we just didn't have many in Sevier County. So here sat this guy with his long hair and beads all around his neck, a beard and sandals. When he spoke he had a very strong Yankee accent.

The gist of the case was that somebody saw this guy driving through Sevierville on his way up into the mountain areas and, of course, they reported it to Bat. Bat had him followed and he had gone way back up in the mountains in the eastern areas of Sevier County and went up a little holler. The defendant had found a place where the road ended with a little cabin that he had obviously gotten the right to use. He stopped and about that time Bat came in behind him in a cruiser.

The defendant was being represented by a New York lawyer who had been flown down here by the American Civil Liberties Union. The defendant, it turned out, was a member of the faculty or staff of Columbia University in New York. As he told his story you could tell that he didn't much expect anybody to believe him. He said that he had been at the cabin only a few minutes and was unloading a few things out of his car when Bat came by himself in a police cruiser. He said Bat got out and talked to him and said he didn't know if he could leave him up there or not, that he was in pretty big trouble. The defendant said he asked what the trouble was and Bat said he didn't know, that it could be a number of things. At that point, he said, Bat went to the sheriff's car and got out a guitar, sat down on a stump and started pickin' and singing some country music. The man said he stood there and watched him. He didn't know what to think about this. He asked again what he and done, and Bat said he was just afraid that the man was in trouble and was in a lot of danger up there.

About that time, the man said, Bat pulled out his pistol and fired two or three rounds up into the air. And then, he said, up in the hills from a couple of other places he heard other gunfire. Bat said, "This is a dangerous place and I'm just going to have to take you in." Then Bat asked the man if he liked country music.

The man said he was afraid to say that he didn't like it, so he told Bat he did, and Bat sat on the stump and picked a couple more songs, then loaded him in the police car, took him in and put him in jail. The man, still not sure what he was being charged with, if anything, got to use the telephone and called the ACLU lawyer in New York.

The strange thing about all of this dialogue that was taking place during this trial was Judge Reagan, who was sitting there on the bench. After I came in he would look back at me every now and then. As I had said, I don't think either the defendant or his lawyer expected people to believe them, but Judge Reagan didn't have any doubt but they were telling substantially the truth and I didn't either. But it was right strange.

So the judge asked Bat exactly where the property was where he had made this arrest. And the lawyer said that it was a non-resident owner that owned the property and had sent this man written permission to use it, and had also sent him a photocopy of his warranty deed. Judge Reagan asked to see the deed, looked at it and said, "Sheriff, this property is in Cocke County. You got over the Sevier County line."

Bat said, well, he didn't know that. It was hard to tell just where the line was up there.

Judge Reagan dismissed the lawsuit and both the lawyer and the defendant were surprised. Bat asked the defendant what he was going to do, and the man replied, "Sheriff, I can tell you right now, I'm going to get out of this place just as soon as I can." Bat Gibson was really a very popular sheriff. People liked him. He had a sense of humor. But he did have a different way of enforcing the law that made for a lot of interesting stories.

One day I walked out of my office going to the courthouse and looked across the street toward the jail and parked in front of the jail was this sheriff's cruiser that had been in a terrible wreck. Obviously, the wrecker had pulled it in and left it there.

I walked on across to look at the car because it was such a very bad wreck, and as I was standing there looking at it Sheriff Bat Gibson came out of the jail and came up to me.

I said, "What happened, Bat? Looks like this one is pretty well torn up."

"Well," he said, "Johnny, you wouldn't believe what happened to that car. Yesterday I was in that car going to Knoxville and as I was on the way down there I had the police radio on and I heard Knox County talking to the City of Knoxville. They were in hot pursuit of a car which they described as heading toward Sevierville on Chapman Highway.

"Just about the time I heard that report, this car comes by me heading towards Sevierville at a very, very fast rate of speed. I made a U-turn and got behind him. I turned on my lights and siren, but he wouldn't stop. I pretty well caught up with him and was behind him and I still couldn't get him to stop, so I took out my pistol and I laid about two over the top of his head. About that time, he pulled in to a picnic area there on the right and I thought, 'Well, I've got this guy stopped.'

"So I got out of the car to approach him and he rolled down a window and shot at me. Of course, he missed me and after he shot he wheeled around and headed back toward Knoxville. Well, that made me pretty mad and I got in my car and started after him again and I told Knoxville on the radio that I was running him back toward Knoxville. About that time he made a U-turn and started back toward Sevierville again. Well, I made another turn and started back after him. We didn't go very far before he turned around again, and I turned around to follow him.

"We was going awful fast, and about that time we got into Knox County there where Earl Good used to have a nightclub on the highway where those beer joints are. Well, Knox County had set up a roadblock with four or five cruisers there, knowing that he was coming that way."

The suspect saw the roadblock and he just pulled over and stopped, but Bat was going way too fast by that time. He was unable to stop and he ran into two or three of those cruisers in that roadblock. He not only tore up the Sevier County Sheriff's cruiser, but severely damaged two or three of the Knox County cruisers as well.

After he told me the story, Bat added, "Can you believe it? They want me to pay for those cars down in Knoxville and there they had them parked in the middle of the road. There wasn't any way for me to stop and get by them!"

During the years that I tried lawsuits I worked with and against some very fine lawyers. I tried many lawsuits against Bob Ogle and many other members of the Sevier County Bar who were practicing at that time, such as the Wynn boys and W. Henry Ogle. In Newport Ed Heard and Ken Porter were both good lawyers. Over in Jefferson County Chester Rainwater (who later became chancellor), B. J. Ramsey and O. D. Bridges were very active in the practice of law.

I was in court in Knoxville quite often and, of course, Knoxville lawyers very frequently came to Sevier County to try lawsuits. Ray and Erby Jenkins, Foster Arnett, Art Byrne, Bob Campbell, Bruce Foster and George Montgomery were very prominent attorneys of that bar. Jack Doughty, Stuart Dye, Frank Flynn and Ben Williamson were good trial lawyers and tried lawsuits all over East Tennessee. George Morton, a member of the Knoxville Bar, is a brilliant lawyer. If you had a case against L. C. Ely you'd better be well prepared.

I was in federal court with Lewis Howard, a good trial lawyer from Knoxville. Irma Greenwood was one of the few women lawyers trying lawsuits at that time.

Over in Maryville, Tennessee, Huston and A. B. Goddard, John and Roy Crawford, Rom Mears and Frank Bird were in the arena.

Our law firm was very successful and I enjoyed working with my partners, who were also very fine lawyers. Pete Hailey was our senior partner. Dennis Jarvis practiced law with us for several years, then Randy Sykes joined the firm, as did Ron Sharp. We had a number of associates who also added a lot of value to our firm. Jim Ripley came with us. Dan Scott tried lawsuits with us for a number of years as well.

Our son, John B. Waters, III, is a lawyer. A nephew, Kenneth Cutshaw, and a niece, Amy Hughes Huskins, are lawyers. I like to think I had some influence in their decisions to enter this noble profession.

The Smoky Mountain Queen underway

The Queen on the Little Pigeon River

Riverboat gamblers on the Queen, left to right: Bill Parsons, Alvin Hodges, Randy Sykes, Bill Stevens, and John B. Waters III holds the royal flush.

SMOKY MOUNTAIN QUEEN

The first settlers in Sevier County made their homes along the French Broad River. Later people moved up the Little Pigeon River and began to settle the farm and excellent bottom land along the Little Pigeon River and the many creeks and branches which fed into the Little Pigeon and the French Broad Rivers.

The early roads were little more than trails. The trails sufficed to get the people into the area. Most early arrivals brought with them very little: a few tools, farm implements, cooking utensils and, of course, their rifles. After the cabin and the barn were built, the land was cleared and planted. Very soon the new settler was producing more than he could eat or market. In addition to the skins, furs, beeswax and forest products, markets were needed for corn, potatoes, whiskey, bacon, cider, tobacco, beef, butter, lard, flour and meal.

Farmers in Sevier County and most other East Tennessee counties began to build flatboats, load their goods and produce, wait for "high water" and start the long hazardous journey downstream to the markets they could find. Many went all the way to New Orleans. When they reached their journey's end, both boat and cargo were sold because the flatboat could not be brought up the river. It had no source of power other than the muscles of the river men on board. The current of the river and everything else floated in the river downstream. From Sevierville to New Orleans the fall was over 900 feet. It was all downbound.

The trip was a holiday for the farmer. Being away from home he would sometimes go a little wild. It was said that men who were decent, quiet deacons at home would throw aside religion and peace when on their annual trip down the river.

The flatboat was a logical craft for the Sevier County skipper. As its name indicated, it was a flat-bottomed boat. Even when fully loaded, it had very little draft and could go very well on the shallow waters of the Little Pigeon and the French Broad. It was constructed of rough-sawed lumber made watertight with coal tar and pitch. The boat was usually ten feet wide and twenty-five to fifty feet in length. A low cabin protected the cargo and boatmen. Shoals were managed by pulling the boat into deeper water by lines and pulleys made fast to trees on the bank. In many instances, a nearby farmer would bring his team of horses or mules into the river to pull the boat off the shoals or shallows. The flatboat was used extensively from the late 1700s to the latter part of the 1800s. Boats left from Sevierville, Catlettsburg and all along the French Broad. Many well-known Sevier County families operated boats. Among them were the Newmans, Atchleys, Brabsons, Maples, Emerts and Catletts.

Ignatius Dyer and his flatboat Good Luck arrived at New Orleans on May 6, 1806. His cargo was thirty-two bales of cotton, five hundred pounds of bacon, two hundred pounds of lard, and forty gallons of whiskey. Dyer had sailed from Sevierville on the Little Pigeon River. (Engineers on the Twin Rivers, U.S. Army Corps of Engineers 1979.)

Brownlow Newman lived on the French Broad River near the Seven Island Community all his life. His father was the well-known Captain Newman who ran steamboats from Knoxville to Dandridge and Sevierville and other points on the French Broad for many years. Brownlow at age 90 told me this flatboat story.

At first the flatboats were small, maybe eight feet wide and ten or twelve feet long, but as the farmer produced more product and had more excess product the flatboats got larger. The farmer needed to get his produce to market and, as he had more of it, he needed a larger boat. If the trip was only to Knoxville the boats returned to Sevierville, especially after the steamboat got to Knoxville. What would happen was that the farmer would load his produce around Catlettsburg (or what was later called Cobbtown) on the flatboat, float it down the French Broad to Knoxville and then very laboriously pole and pull the flatboat back upstream to Sevierville.

Brownlow said the flatboats of that time were often named after the man who built the boat. The boat known as the Maples was built by a man named Maples, the Whaley built by Whaley, and so forth.

When Brownlow was a very small boy the need arose for bigger boats. A man named John Maples was known as Big John. He was a carpenter and had built boats before, and he built the biggest boat used yet out of Sevierville. It was known as the Big John. It was probably ten by forty feet long. Brownlow said a big boy who had never been out of Sevier County worked for his father, Captain Newman, and the boy was on the Big John when she made her first trip to Knoxville carrying a large load of hams, hides, and Brownlow said, maybe some whiskey.

The boat tied up at Knoxville next to a steamboat and offloaded the cargo. The captain of the steamboat came to the side of his steamboat and, looking down on the flatboat, said, "You boys get unloaded and move your little boat over to the bank out of the way."

The boy, Brownlow said, with a very surprised look, looked at Brownlow and said, "Little boat! My God, don't he know this is the Big John?"

In 1839 a newspaper account in the Knoxville Gazette noted that over one hundred boats would leave Knoxville bound for New Orleans and markets downstream that spring when the spring tides came and, as the article said, "the waters answering."

In 1974 the Sevier County Bicentennial Committee was formed to make plans for the celebration of the nation's 200th birthday, to be celebrated in 1976. One of the first approved projects was the flatboat. It was decided that a flatboat would be built at Sevierville and make the trip down the Little Pigeon River into the French Broad and Tennessee River to Knoxville and other towns and cities downstream. The boat was to be built similarly to those that early Sevier County citizens operated and was to carry a cargo typical of that shipped by early settlers.

I presented the flatboat proposal to the Bicentennial Committee and was asked to head the project. We got a little press about the idea and men began to contact me and say they would like to be included among the volunteers and we got under way.

On Saturday night, April 24, 1976, a big celebration was held at the Sevier County Fairgrounds where the flatboat, the Smoky Mountain Queen, had been built. The boat was ready and plans were to get under way the next morning on Sunday, April 25, at which time the boat would be launched on the Little Pigeon River and commence its downstream journey.

The late winter and spring of 1976 was unusually dry. We had little rain during the months when we generally had a lot of rain. The Little Pigeon was very low and the French Broad had little water running in it except from streams that came in below Douglas Dam, and really not much water unless water was released from Douglas Dam when the dam was running its generators. I was aware that we were going to have a problem floating the Queen down the French Broad over a number of shoals. I went to my friend, Red Wagner, who was then chairman of TVA, and told him my problem. We wanted to launch the boat on a Sunday morning. Red was well aware of the shoals and places where the water was very shallow. "When do you want the water, John?" Red asked.

"Red, I want it at 9 a.m. on Sunday, with the French Broad banks as full as possible."

The newspaper and radio were giving the Queen a lot of publicity and a lot of people were planning to watch us get under way that morning. I began to get telephone calls early in the week.

"Johnny, there's no way that boat's going to go down the French Broad River. The water is way too low."

People were also saying the same thing to the crew members.

"Don't worry," I said, "we'll have water."

Well, you can imagine some of the looks and comments I got in response to that statement. My reputation in Sevier County went up several points at exactly 9 a.m. when the water started rising in the French Broad and we had plenty of water to get to Knoxville those next few days.

Little did I realize at that time in 1976 that thirteen years later I would again witness the power of TVA in controlling the river system. In 1989 Knoxville Mayor Victor Ashe asked Bobby Congleton and me to be co-chairmen of a Bicentennial Celebration for the City of Knoxville and to set up a birthday party for the city. One of the things that was suggested was to get some of the big paddlewheel steamboats that do cruises on the river to come to Knoxville. Such an event had been done in Cincinnati and was very popular. Four or five big steamboats came there and added a lot to the birthday celebration for Cincinnati. The mayor and others who were working on this project contacted a man up in Cincinnati who had been active in this and knew about the operation of the steamboats. They invited him to come down to Knoxville and meet with the Knoxville Bicentennial Committee. Carolyn (Mrs. Tom) Jensen was very active on this committee and she later told me this story in more detail than what I had witnessed.

At that time I was a director of the Tennessee Valley Authority. We were having this meeting and talking about bringing these steamboats up to Knoxville for the celebration and this man said, "Well, you've got a big problem. There's two boats that we might be able to get, but there's no way you can get them to Knoxville. You can't get them under these bridges. You lack a couple of feet. Their masts are too high to get under the railroad and the bridge here at Knoxville. I could get two of these boats down here, I think, but there's just no way they could get into Knoxville."

So I said, "Well, you make the arrangements to get the boats and you let me know when they're coming, and I'll have the water down so that they can come under the bridge."

Well, we adjourned, and Carolyn Jensen said this man said, "Who does this guy think he is and what does he think he is going to do?"

Carolyn laughed and said, "Well, he's a director of TVA. If he wants to lower the Tennessee River here at Knoxville he can do it."

The man said, "Well, I've never had any experience with this. It's a new experience for me."

Of course, once again, just opening the gates at Fort Loudon Dam easily let the water down two feet to let the boats through.

At the request of Judge Ray L. Reagan., county judge of Sevier County, Tennessee, I had prepared a document to serve as greetings to our downstream visitors that we would call on along the way. The document, signed by Ray Reagan, is as follows:

To all forts, stations, towns, villages, militia, boatmen, settlers, friendly Indians and others downstream from Sevierville, Tennessee, on the Little Pigeon River, the French Broad, the Tennessee, the Ohio, and the Mississippi Rivers: Greetings.

The Sevier County flatboat, "Smoky Mountain Queen," is scheduled to depart Sevierville, on April 25, 1976, subject to the waters of the Little Pigeon River and the French Broad answering. The "Queen" and her crew of Sevier Countians seek to recreate the trip made by early settlers of our county when the goods and produce of the county were shipped to down river markets by flatboat. It is a project of the SEVIER COUNTY AMERICAN REVOLUTION BICENTENNIAL COMMITTEE. The people of Sevier County invite all down river people and lowlanders to participate in this project as a part of our celebration of the Nation's 200th Birthday.

Therefore, I, Ray L. Reagan, as County Judge of Sevier County, Tennessee, and chief administrative officer of The Sevier County settlement, do commend to you the Smoky Mountain Queen and her crew and ask safe passage for boat, crew and cargo through your territorial waters.

You are further requested:
1) To notify, order, request or direct your officials, citizens and residents to join in the festivities and celebration of this Bicentennial event and render all reasonable and necessary assistance for the good boat, "Smoky Mountain Queen," should she survive the perilous and hazardous trip to your waterways and banks.

2) To overlook the minor indiscretions or law violations Which may be committed by the boat's crew, realizing that Said crew is made up of brave, even courageous men from Sevier County, who may, at times, be carried away with the festive occasion and temporarily disregard their Puritan and strict upbringing —remembering at all times that their wives and children are fearfully awaiting their return home from their perilous trip.

Signed, Ray L. Reagan
County Judge, Sevier County, Tennessee

The flatboat, Smoky Mountain Queen, was constructed of a marine plywood hull which had a layer of fiberglass over it. The boat was ten feet wide and thirty feet long. The boat was visually authentic in every way. On the outside was rough-sawed lumber. The seams between the boards were caulked with "oakum" fiber and tar. The hull was well-built and safe. The boat was powered by two fifty-horse outboard Johnson motors. The Tennessee River had very little current since nine dams have been built on the river by the Tennessee Valley Authority. So there was no current to push the boat downstream as the early settlers had relied on. A small cabin was built on the boat and you stepped down into the boat a couple of feet so the cabin protruded up above the deck only about four or five feet. A pot-bellied stove furnished heat for the cabin. On the back deck was a coop with nine hens and one rooster. The rooster was named Rudy and became the Queen's mascot. The boat was built at the Sevier County Fairgrounds and about twenty-five men worked on the boat from time to time.

On May 29, 1976, at 1 p.m., the Smoky Mountain Queen arrived at the port of New Orleans. On board were nine hens, one rooster and seventeen men. The boat had traveled sixteen hundred miles, been through nine states and taken thirty-five days to make the trip. The boat had crossed the state of Tennessee three times and descended from nine hundred feet altitude at Sevierville to sea level at New Orleans.

The men who actually built the flatboat at the Sevier County Fairgrounds were certainly not boat builders, even though they had a variety of skills. They were all volunteers and they worked for months in their spare time on the boat. Bill Parsons was the chief engineer and designer of the boat. Bill was a good craftsman and was certainly the leading expert on how to design and build a boat. And the fact that the boat was very seaworthy and easy to handle was due to his design, which he developed as the project went along. A set of plans on paper never really existed. Randy Sykes did a lot of work in getting supplies and materials needed for construction. He also helped raise donated funds needed to buy supplies. Pete Hailey also helped in this regard. The late Bill Blackwell was a very important person in the building of the boat. Bill furnished a lot of muscle and brains and was among the first of the group to put forth the idea that the boat must really go all the way to New Orleans. It was a real shock to the crew when Bill Blackwell had a heart attack and died while working on the Queen. His death, instead of casting a pall on the project, made the crew even more determined to complete the project and dedicate the Queen to Bill Blackwell's memory.

Among other people who worked on the boat were Bill Stevens, Dr. Leroy Dyer, Richard Lykens, John B. Waters III, Alvin Hodges, Harold Romines, Bud Copeland, Marc Cardoso, Jack Summerfield, Kenneth Cutshaw, Fred Raymond, Porter Fox and Al Schmutzer, Jr.

Bill Stevens was officially the "Voice of the Queen." Bill had some experience in television and radio broadcasting and he used the radio transmitter provided by radio station WSEV to make reports back to the radio station on the progress of the Queen. These reports became very popular. After we got too far down the river for the radio transmitter, they were made periodically by telephone back to the radio station.

In addition to the men on the crew, the Queen had two cabin boys, Chris Sykes and Dale Romines. The crew also had an official photographer who unexpectedly showed up one day at the work site and went along on the trip. His name was Mike Hoban and he made a lot of pictures. John B. Waters III dropped out of the University of Tennessee temporarily and was the only person to go every inch of the way from the time the boat left Sevierville via the Little Pigeon until it arrived at New Orleans.

The Bicentennial Committee had notified Bicentennial Committees downriver, giving them times when the Queen expected to stop at their city. Each night the Queen would tie up and would be under way only in the daytime. When it stopped at night, many of the Bicentennial Committees along the way would hold celebrations, parties and functions for the crew. One crew member said that he had never eaten so much fried chicken and barbecue in his life. As you might guess, the crew was very well entertained along the way by the towns the crew visited. At every stop the Queen's theme was "Happy Birthday, America." When the Queen got ready to get under way again, "God Bless America" was always sung by the crew and all visitors who were there to see the departure.

Fred Raymond, John Sonner and Ron Sharp, along with Lynn Webb and Jack McGlynn, were on board on various legs of the trip. There were generally five to eight crew members on board at any one time. A station wagon was generally en route back and forth from Sevierville to the Queen. The crew members had grown beards and had dress similar to what early boatmen might have worn.

On the third day under way the Smoky Mountain Queen arrived at Knoxville, Tennessee, at Knoxville's Bicentennial Boat Dock on the Tennessee

River. The Queen arrived at noon and more than two hundred Sevier and Knox County citizens were there to greet the crew. Many yachts and boats came up the river to meet the Queen to escort her in to the dock at Knoxville. Greeting the flatboat was Mayor Randy Tyree, who presented the crew with a proclamation, and in return received a "jug of Smoky Mountain 'shine." Red Wagner, Chairman of TVA, and Ed Boling, president of the University of Tennessee, were also present.

After the Queen departed Knoxville on April 27, she arrived at Kingston on April 28, Spring City April 29, and Decatur on the 30th. On Saturday, May 1, the Queen arrived at Chattanooga and spent the night at Loret Villa, where many people from Sevier County came to join in the Chattanooga celebration. The Queen got under way on Sunday, May 2 and on Monday, May 3 was in Bridgeport, Alabama. On Wednesday the 5th the Queen was at Guntersville, Alabama; on the 6th in Decatur, Alabama; and on the 7th in Florence, Alabama. The Queen started its trip on the northbound leg of the Tennessee on Sunday, May 9, which was Mother's Day.

We locked through the Pickwick Lock on Mother's Day. It was a beautiful day and there was tremendous boat traffic on the river at that time. We had to wait several hours before we were able to lock the Smoky Mountain Queen through the lock and get on our way. This made us run quite a bit late that day and I happened to be running the boat at that particular time. We were concerned because we weren't going to be able to get to Clifton during daylight hours, where we wanted to spend that night. We had never planned to be under way with the Smoky Mountain Queen at night and we didn't have the proper running lights for night traffic.

I was talking on the marine radio to a towboat captain who had locked through with us. He was pushing six or eight barges. These towboat captains are very interesting people and unbelievably cooperative and helpful, and they were always interested when they saw the Smoky Mountain Queen, wanting to know what we were doing and who we were and where we were going. We always identified ourselves over the marine radio as "the Sevier County Bicentennial flatboat, the Smoky Mountain Queen." These captains were extremely helpful people and always gave us good advice, telling us how to stay in safe water when they were passing. Of course, a big towboat pushing a big tow ahead would create a tremendous wake and what they call a rooster tail, a big, high spurt of water behind that comes out of those powerful screws when the towboat pushes a very heavy load.

Anyway, I was talking to this captain on this towboat and I said, "We're wanting to get to Clifton tonight and we're running late because we were so late locking through and I don't think we're going to make it. How far is it to Clifton?"

Well, he told us and indicated that we were looking at ten or eleven o'clock at night to get to Clifton, and then he said, "I tell you what. You won't have any trouble. You just fall in behind me and I'll watch out for you and keep you informed of what we're doing."

I said, "Well, Captain, that's really nice. I appreciate it. I think that's what we're going to do."

Then in another minute, he came back up on the air and he said, "If you're really worried about this situation, you just come on up alongside my first barge and I'll have a crane lift you on board and we'll just haul you down to Clifton and set you off."

We got a real kick out of realizing that they had the capability of doing that. At any rate, that night when we got to Clifton, he said he would show us where to enter the little harbor at Clifton, since the entrance was pretty narrow. They had unbelievable candlepower on those towboats and he lit that thing up as if it was noon. We tied up at a pier and spent the night at Clifton, which is a very well-known, old river town that has a lot of history behind it. It was an interesting place to stop.

On the tenth we were at Perryville, the eleventh at Birdsong near Camden, and on May 15 the boat arrived at Paducah, Kentucky.

All along the way the ship's crew kept a detailed log of events that occurred, and for each leg of the journey there was a captain in charge. This was an individual named to be in charge of the boat for a particular time.

On Sunday, May 16 the Queen got under way from Paducah, Kentucky, at 9:10 in the morning. At 9:35 the Queen entered the Ohio River. It was raining and at 10:25, the Queen locked into Dam Number Fifty-Two on the Ohio. At 12:30 the log says the rain stopped, tarps were removed and smooth sailing, but stiff breezes faced the boat during the next two hours. The boat was being piloted by Porter Fox and the log says the wind blew mattresses off the topside. Fortunately two fishermen who recognized the boat approached, picked up the mattresses and returned them. At 16:00 the boat tied up at Cairo, Illinois. The next day, May 17, at 9:27 the Queen was under way from Cairo. The crew was cleaning up the results of the bad weather. At 9:41, the log says as follows, "Entered the Mississippi River and through the glorious river's mud and foggy sky, we came about and steamed up the Mississippi to meet the Bicentennial Wagon Train which was being off-loaded from a barge crossing the Mississippi." The log notes at 12:05 that they passed the Cale, a three-stacker tug pushing twenty-six barges. They passed in a narrow channel. "We had a good ride but no problems. Large swell from the tug." At 12:30 the log says, "The first card game on the Mississippi. Porter Fox, Doug Munson, and John Waters, III are now Mississippi riverboat gamblers." At 14:30 the log says, "Passed three-stacker tug pushing twenty-three barges in a narrow channel. Shook our teeth. Seven-foot breakers."

At 7:15 they beached on a mud bank near New Madrid, hitched a ride into town, borrowed three gas cans, and made two trips hauling gas. Starboard and port both took twelve and a half gallons. At 22:00 the whole crew turned in after a meal of chili.

"Thursday, May 18, 6:15. Smoky Mountain Queen under way. A beautiful day."

"On Thursday May 16 at 10:40 in the morning the Smoky Mountain Queen met another queen, perhaps somewhat more famous, the famous Delta Queen, old time paddle-wheeler that runs the Mississippi up and down hauling guests. Big crowd. Several toured the Smoky Mountain Queen."

During this leg of the journey John B. Waters, III was captain in charge. At 11:40 on Wednesday, May 19, the Queen docked at the Memphis Yacht Club. The whole crew got showers, made an official entry into Memphis and was greeted by a big delegation including the mayor, Bicentennial chairman, and a number of members of the judiciary. A big day."

I had a lawsuit scheduled to try in the Circuit Court of Sevier County and had not been able to be on board the Queen any time during its journey on the Mississippi River. So I was really very pleased when my lawsuit was compromised and settled and I did not have to try what I thought might be a two- or three-day lawsuit. I knew that the Queen was scheduled to get in to Baton Rouge, Louisiana, and I was able to make arrangements to fly down there and join the crew at Baton Rouge. On Wednesday, May 26, the Queen's log states that the Queen got under way at 6:14, leaving Natches Under the Hill. The log said that at 8:15 they had breakfast prepared and served by

Fred Raymond, which was fried eggs, bacon and coffee. About ten o'clock that morning the log states that they began to encounter very high winds from the south. At noon they stopped at Angola Ferry to ask about weather conditions. The ferryman gave them a bad forecast. He said rain and high winds were predicted downstream. They got underway from Angola Ferry and, sure enough, they encountered a lot of high winds and rough water. Although they had not seen any rain as yet by noon, they saw the roughest water encountered so far. They covered the foredeck with tarps. About a little after 1 o'clock, they encountered the towboat, Biglow, and talked with the pilot. They had passed this pilot earlier around Memphis, and he kindly offered any assistance needed. He said that nasty weather would be very likely from here on down. They talked to Captain Leroy Dyer a lot over the radio. At 1400 hours, the log said Johnny B. Waters prepared fried Spam and beans for lunch, then the weather began to clear and they got into Red's Boat Dock at Baton Rouge.

After they left Natches, Mississippi, the log says that two new crew members, Dr. John Sonner and Lynn Webb, came on board from Sevierville. This was a long day for the Queen. She was under way thirteen hours and covered 130 miles, which was the longest day yet for the Queen and included very rough weather, high winds, and some rain. The log then states that this is where I got on board with Rick Lykens.

The Baton Rouge papers were really covering the Queen. They had a big article that morning. TV stations also came down and filmed the Queen and the log says that when they laid over at Red's Boat Dock at Baton Rouge they made two runs for the TV stations. What would happen is that the TV stations wanted the boat to go back out and come back into the landing at Baton Rouge so they could film the arrival and the crew was always glad to do this. The log also mentions that they went into Baton Rouge to a great restaurant, the Giamancho, that night and had Cajun food.

The next day on Friday, we got under way really early from Red's Boat Dock. The log states that at 6 o'clock we passed a Turkish Merchant Marine vessel anchored in the river. This was the first ocean-going vessel that the Queen had seen that had come this far up the Mississippi. Of course, they may come further up, but this was the first one that the Queen had encountered. Later we began to pass more ocean vessels, including a merchant vessel, the Pan America, at anchor. That evening at 1640 hours (4:30 P.M.

on twelve-hour time) the Queen docked beside the Destrehan Ferry at Destrehan, Louisiana.

The next morning, a Saturday, we got under way from Destrehan and on board were Crew Captain Leroy Dyer; my son, John B. Waters, III; myself; Rick Lykens, John Sonner; Fred Raymond; Mike Hoban, the photographer; and Randy and Chris Sykes; Harold Romines and Bill Parsons. Alvin Hodges also came on board. The log noted that we were twenty-six miles from New Orleans, Louisiana. We began to hear communicating over the marine radio some of the Cajun riverboat pilots on the river in this particular area. Of course, the Cajun people have a wonderful accent, a mixture of French, English and I don't know what else, but I was very interested hearing two Cajun pilots talk to each other about seeing us on the river. One pilot was asking the other, "Have you seen dat funny looking boat on the river?"

And the other one said, "Yeah, yeah, I see dat boat."

The first said, "What is it?"

The second Cajun had heard us talking on the radio and, as mentioned before, we always identified ourselves as "We are the Sevier County Bicentennial flatboat, the Smoky Mountain Queen."

So this second Cajun pilot was telling his friend, yes, he had seen the boat and he had heard us on the radio, and he said, "Dis boat is a unusual looking boat. It's one of these Bisexual Boats." I guess that was a misunderstanding of the word, Bicentennial, from that captain's point of view.

On May 29 the Smoky Mountain Queen arrived in New Orleans. About fifty or sixty people had flown down from Sevier County to meet the Queen and a big celebration was had. Senator Hank Larcella, a state senator in Louisiana and former All-American football player for the University of Tennessee, had arranged a big celebration. The brass band was there and a number of dignitaries from New Orleans greeted the Queen.

Remarks I made on the arrival of the Queen in New Orleans stated the following: "The people of Sevier County, Tennessee have sent this flatboat, the Smoky Mountain Queen, to you, the people of New Orleans, to bring you a message. The message is 'Happy Birthday, America.' In this Bicentennial year, Sevier County, Tennessee, wanted to recreate the spirit of early Americans. They wanted to demonstrate the fact that Americans still possess the thrill of adventure, the ingenuity and courage of our early settlers and pioneers. They wanted to know if the spirit of cooperation and hospitality could be rekindled. For one hundred and fifty years the people on the river assisted the upland people as thousands of flatboats came down the river to your city with their cargoes of goods and produce. Would the descendants of these people extend their hands in help and friendship? The answer is a resounding, 'Yes.' Love of country, pride of heritage, the desire to be a good neighbor, these characteristics exist the same in the heart of the man from the mountains as from the man from the river. All along the way the crew of the Smoky Mountain Queen found these beautiful traits in the people in this great Heart of America."

On June 7, 1976, the United States Army Engineers returned the Queen to Sevierville, Tennessee, on a lowboy tractor trailer. A welcome home party was held at the Court House in Sevierville, at 4:30 p.m., Monday, June 27, 1976.

Senator Jennings Randolph, D-W VA, JBW, Sen. Howard Baker,
Supreme Court Justice Potter Stewart

President Nixon signing the Appalachian Bill. From left to right, Senator Howard Baker, Senator Jennings Randolph, Vice President Spiro Agnew, Senator Montoya from New Mexico, Senator Cook from Kentucky, and JBW in Oval Office.

JBW and President Richard Nixon in the Oval Office

APPALACHIAN REGIONAL COMMISSION

After President Richard Nixon was elected, Howard Baker called me in the early part of 1969 and asked me to consider being appointed as the federal co-chairman of the Appalachian Regional Commission. I was practicing law at the time in Sevierville and our children were twelve and fourteen years of age. Going to Washington was really not on my schedule at that particular time; however, I simply couldn't resist the opportunity to go to Washington and see how the "Big Boys" operated politically and in government. So I told Howard I would be delighted to get that position. I knew something about the Appalachian Commission, but not much, but I certainly did considerable research after that call.

President Nixon nominated me on Senator Baker's recommendation and I was confirmed by the United States Senate on March 26, 1969. Justice Potter Stewart of the United States Supreme Court administered the oath to me in a ceremony Senator Baker hosted in the United States Capitol.

Patsy and I decided that we wouldn't actually move the family to Washington, but I would get a two-bedroom apartment so that we could have the children there a lot and they could have the opportunity to learn about the nation's capital. The apartment was on Calvert Street, which is just off of Connecticut Avenue, actually kind of in between where the Shorham Hotel is over on the other side of Calvert and the Washington Sheraton, then known as the Sheraton Park. Patsy and the children came up quite often and spent time in Washington, and both Johnny B. and Cyndy learned a great deal about the capital while I was there.

The Appalachian Regional Development Act was passed in 1965. The act was a response to the persistent economic and social hardships that blighted the lives of so many who lived in the Appalachian area. This distress was largely rooted in the sharp decline in mining, agriculture and railroad employment as technology and market conditions changed rapidly during the 1950s. In that decade the people of Appalachia lost over half the jobs in agriculture and almost 60 percent of the jobs in mining. Railroad employment, a major source of jobs in many parts of Appalachia, dropped by 40 percent. This economic distress was compounded by the physical isolation of a large part of the region. Rugged mountains and narrow valleys characterize the core of Appalachia. The lack of adequate highways handicapped development of the region as nationally increasing commerce moved by road had simply skirted the mountainous regions of the Appalachians.

Under the act the commission was made up of the entire state of West Virginia and parts of twelve other states: Alabama, Georgia, Kentucky, Maryland, Mississippi, New York, North Carolina, Ohio, Pennsylvania, South Carolina, Tennessee and Virginia. The commission members were the governors of these thirteen states, with the Appalachian Regional Commission federal co-chairman, the job that I had, serving as the federal voice on the commission with an absolute veto over any measures the commission adopted. The term "Co-Chairman" was used because we always had a states co-chairman, a position that rotated among the member governors periodically. The idea was that at one meeting of the commission, the states co-chairman (one of the governors) would preside, and at the next meeting the federal co-chairman would preside. The governors appointed what was called state representatives, and they did the staff work and main work representing the governors on the commission.

The commission engaged in a broad spectrum of economic development programs, including the construction of development highways, health facilities, vocational education, sewer and water projects, land reclamation, housing and the supplementation of other federal grant and aid programs. The commission actually built nothing. Construction was always turned over to the agency, either state or federal, that was more equipped to do that. But the commission set up criteria and funding for these programs. Each state was required to present a plan to the commission for the development of the resources which the commission funded, and this plan was approved by the commission staff, and then projects in the plan could be funded during that particular year.

Having been born and reared in Sevier County, I certainly had first-hand experience with a number of the problems that affected the entire region, even though in Sevier County we never had a coal economy. But we did have the mountains, and with the blessing of the beautiful mountains we also had the isolation that the mountains bring. The construction of roads was very difficult, and yet highway access in and out of a region and access to other markets was terribly important for the development of the region. I'm really proud of some of the things the commission has done over the years in the road development program.

We were also keenly aware of the nature of the people who lived in the Appalachian Mountains. They are a proud, independent people. They're bound to the land and to their past by a strong sense of place and belonging. They are people who tend to regard the rest of the world with equal parts of shyness and sometimes suspicion. Consequently, the Appalachian program was designed as an experiment in government, with the state and federal governments as partners.

One of the programs which I was deeply involved in during my tenure as federal co-chairman was the Vocational Education Program. Prior to the commission, most of the vocational education in high schools in the region was strictly agricultural. Our people were taught how to farm. The problem was there were generally very few jobs in agriculture in the region and farming had rapidly lost out to the big farm belt areas to the west and south of the region, and yet we still taught vocational agriculture. We adopted a position at the commission that we would fund only vocational training that was job-related. The state had to come up with a plan that proved that there were jobs in the area and we would then fund vocational training to allow for those jobs. It was very rewarding to see the interest of some of these young people in learning skills, and vocational training in the Appalachian Region has been a major factor in increasing the quality of life for so many people who live in the region. During 1969 while I was federal co-chairman, we funded fifty-nine vocational and technical schools in the region that provided facilities for thirty-four-thousand students.

The commission also made good progress that year in highway construction and certain health facilities were improved or provided. One of the things that I was extremely interested in, and which I regret was not as successful as I would have liked, was setting up a child development program. President Nixon was interested in child development and this was one of those areas where historically there were two branches of government (state and federal) that had addressed part of these problems. Certainly education was a big factor in child development: educating parents, pre-natal care, education of the children themselves.

Health was the other side of the problem, because so many of the children were under-nourished. They didn't have the proper inoculations for the prevention of disease, and even parasite infestations, worms, were a big problem in the Appalachian Region. Getting the public health people and the public education people to cooperate turned out to be a problem that really I found very irritating and distressing. Both sides wanted all the money. This is one of the things you learn in working in government: the sections of government don't like to let other sections be involved. So in this instance, if we were going to have a good child development program, we needed good cooperation between a number of different branches of the government and this was very difficult to do. I think it's still a problem. A good child development program must, of course, include family planning before the child is born, care during pregnancy, care for the child after birth but before school, and early education such as kindergarten and early elementary schools to carry on and eventually give a child an opportunity to be healthy, educated and possess skill or knowledge that will allow him or her to have a good job and support his or her families in the way that we all want.

One of the things the commission attempted to address was simply the cooperation or partnership of state and federal efforts and agencies, and the cooperation of different agencies within the federal government. Many people in highway construction and design did not consider roads as a development tool. This shocked me because, having lived in Appalachia and in the mountains, I knew all my life how important a road was for the development of an area. A road was not simply a way to move people from Point A to Point B, as so many in the federal and state departments of transportation insisted was the case. Almost anyone who ever came to the commission realized what a wonderful advantage we could have if we could have a more regional approach to our problems and the development of our country. Consider how the country was developed and consider the fact that there are some three thousand counties in the United States, as well as, of course, the forty-eight contiguous states. Consider how these state and county lines were drawn. One of the early considerations in the establishment of a county was that a person anywhere in the county could ride on horseback and get to the county seat and return within one day. So, there is very little reason in the way state and county lines were established. This has been a tremendous obstacle in the economic development of the nation.

What we proposed in the Appalachian Regional Commission was that the United States be divided into ten regions, and that economic development be approached in each region. This was then touted as "Wall-to-Wall Appalachia," which then got a lot of political heat and actually went nowhere. But it could have been a big improvement in the way state and federal governments address development issues in their various regions. Unfortunately, it has never been given a chance and I think we've lost because that regional concept has failed. Many pointed out that the Appalachian Region was not really a true region. A more true region would have been the Southern Appalachian Region. But this was because of the politics that created the boundaries of the region when it was formed.

I certainly believed that a great deal could have been done if we had had more regionalism. To me, perhaps the most perfect region is the watershed. If you take the watershed of fairly good-sized rivers, and certainly the watershed of major rivers, you get a region that has a great deal of kinship in terms of problems and development opportunities. I think a great deal could have been done and I tried to get President Nixon to consider establishing the ten regions throughout the United States, and using this as a basis for economic development. He did consider the idea. We met in Louisville one time and presented the idea to him and I thought he listened very favorably. He went on to the West for a ball game in either California or Washington, and he met with some governors out there informally and proposed the plan to them. Unfortunately, these governors didn't understand the concept and there was the idea then that all governors wanted what were called block grants. Uncle Sam should just send the money. This was not going to happen and the idea soon lost its backing. But the concept of regional government has never been tried and I think the country could have been well-served had an attempt been made to approach a number of problems and issues on a regional basis.

I enjoyed my two years in Washington as federal co-chairman. I served until March of 1971, when I resigned and returned to Sevierville to resume my law practice and business. I was fortunate enough to meet a number of governors, the thirteen governors of the Appalachian states, and members of the House and Senate. Senator Jennings Randolph from West Virginia was a strong leader in Appalachia, as was the then junior senator, Senator Bird from West Virginia. Of course, Senator Baker was a very strong leader in public works then, and in Appalachia, and he gave me the opportunity through him to meet and work with a number of other senators. Senator John Sherman Cooper from Kentucky was a very interesting man whom I met and admired. He was also very influential in the Appalachian Commission.

Alabama generally had strong people that supported the commission. Congressman Tom Bevill and Congressman Robert E. Jones are two examples of very powerful members of Congress that strongly supported the commission. While I was there, Robert Jones was chairman of public works. I got well acquainted with Congressman Jones and was very fond of him because he was a very up-front kind of a guy. He always told you exactly where you stood and what was going on. I recall a story about an event that happened while I was there. President Nixon's second term was coming up and the Democrats met in convention and nominated Senator George McGovern from South Dakota as their candidate. Senator McGovern was a very liberal man. Congressman Jones had a more middle-of-the-road or conservative standing. I recall the day after the Democratic Convention, I was in Jones's office and when I walked in he said, "Well, John, I just got off the telephone with a very good friend, a long-standing Democrat from Alabama. He called me up on the phone after the Democratic Convention had nominated McGovern and he said, 'Bob, are you still a Democrat?'"

"My response to him, John, was, 'Yes, I'm a very still Democrat.'"

During those years the state of Georgia had a very unusual man as governor: Lester Maddox. Governor Maddox had been in the restaurant business and was famous for his chicken down in the Atlanta area. He was a very controversial man. You never knew exactly what he was going to say, but he had a lot of humor and it was always interesting to be around him. He was a smarter man than his image projected to the public.

The State of Mississippi was also one of the more active states in the commission, led by Senator John Stennis, an outstanding United States senator who served for many years. One of the most powerful men in the Congress was Congressman Jamie L. Whitten, a democrat from Mississippi. Later when I was at TVA Mr. Whitten was chairman of the House Appropriations Committee.

I enjoyed very much my opportunity to get acquainted with Governor Nelson Rockefeller, who was Governor of New York at that point in time. I wouldn't say that I became a very close personal friend of Governor Rockefeller, but I had the opportunity to be with him on two or three occasions and I enjoyed knowing him. He was a very fine man and unusual man, and I think a man who could have made a great president of the United States had he ever gotten the opportunity.

The Appalachian governors would meet at the same time as the Southern governors held their meeting. The Southern Governors Association was a strong association, and certain numbers of the southern governors were Appalachian governors.

When we would meet, we would generally invite the governors of New York, Pennsylvania and Ohio to come down and meet with the Appalachian governors, and this worked out to be more convenient for everybody, so we often had meetings of the Appalachian governors in conjunction with the Southern Governors Association Meeting.

One particular year the southern governors were meeting in Williamsburg, Virginia, at a beautiful resort that was funded primarily by the Rockefeller family. This particular year Winthrop Rockefeller was governor of Arkansas and he was in line to become the next chairman of the Southern Governor's Conference, so he was hosting the event at Williamsburg, and I must say that Patsy and I have never before or since enjoyed any banquet-type meeting better than we did there. Governor Winthrop Rockefeller spared no expense or effort to have a fantastically wonderful meeting, which we were privileged to attend. When the meeting began, Governor Nelson Rockefeller, of course, from New York, was not a member of the Southern Governor's Conference, so he just flew in for our particular Appalachian meeting, and I went out in a car with a Virginia State Police trooper to pick up Governor Nelson Rockefeller at the airport, because he was only going to be there for the Appalachian Regional Commission part of that event. I went out and picked him up at his airplane, and we got in the car. All these governors had flown into Williamsburg and their airplanes were sitting around on the tarmac all over the fairly small airport. We got in the car and there was a brand new, shiny, beautiful jet, the largest jet in the area, sitting there. Governor Nelson Rockefeller said, "My goodness, whose airplane is that?"

Well, I had asked the same question as we had gone out there and knew the answer, and I said, "Governor, that's the governor of Arkansas' plane."

I never will forget the amusement that Nelson showed as he smiled and shook his head. He said, "Well, Win always did love airplanes!"

I thought, "Well, I guess that's one advantage to being a Rockefeller."

Another rather strange thing happen as we were in the back of that car riding in to the Williamsburg area. I noticed two things about Governor Rockefeller that really surprised me. Near the left knee of his trouser was a darned place, a place where a hole had obviously been torn or worn through the fabric of his trousers, and it had been darned. Also I noticed his shoes were a wing-type shoe and were fairly old. As a matter of fact, they had slight cracks across the tops of the shoes showing wear, and I couldn't help but notice that they had been half-soled. Knowing the wealth of the Rockefeller family, this was surprising. He was a very fine man and his wealth obviously was important to him, but I think he handled it very well.

I recall my first meeting with Governor Rockefeller, even before I went to the Appalachian Regional Commission. During the 1968 presidential elections, Governor Rockefeller was a candidate for the nomination that Richard Nixon eventually won. The convention that year was in Miami, Florida, and I was elected as a delegate from Tennessee. Nixon was the strong man at that time. There were two people in the wings to give him opposition, one being Governor Nelson Rockefeller, and the other the Governor of California, Governor Ronald Reagan. But before the convention was to meet, all the delegates from Tennessee got an invitation to come to Nashville to a hotel near the Nashville Airport for a reception for Governor Nelson Rockefeller to meet him. I decided to go down because I wanted to meet the governor. I had always admired him. I was talking to my father before I went down there, and I said, "I'm going to go down to Nashville and meet Governor Nelson Rockefeller. I don't think he's got much chance to be nominated. It looks like Richard Nixon has got the nomination pretty well sewed up, but I want to go down and meet Governor Rockefeller."

And my father said, "Indeed, you should go down and meet Governor Rockefeller, and when you shake hands with Governor Rockefeller, you thank him for the $5 million that his father, John D. Rockefeller, gave to establish the Great Smoky Mountains National Park, and you tell him how much you appreciate that."

Well, I remembered that when I was standing in line to go through the receiving line to shake hands with the Governor, and when I got to him I said that to him, and I was surprised at his reaction. He obviously appreciated the remark and after I went on through and was standing around talking, as you do, just chit-chatting, we came together again, and he said to me, "Mr. Waters, I appreciate your remark about the Great Smoky Mountains National Park. Not many people remember those things, and I appreciate your remembering that."

It made an impression on him and I think it started off our relationship, because he mentioned that again later when I was at the Appalachian Regional Commission.

Another governor that I enjoyed working with and got well acquainted with was Governor James A. Rhodes, a Republican from Ohio. Governor Rhodes was one of the best politicians I ever met. He knew how to work a crowd. One time I went out with him to dedicate a vocational education school, and we were in his plane and flew around a number of stops. I saw him operate and he was a very skilled politician, never losing the opportunity to talk to the public, and yet moving very quickly through crowds. He was extremely interested in vocational education, so we both shared that interest and got along pretty well with it.

Another governor that I enjoyed working with was Governor Robert E. McNair, a Democrat from South Carolina. Governor McNair was very interested in the commission and was a very smart man, a quick study. I enjoyed working with him a lot.

While I was in the commission, Buford Ellington was governor of the State of Tennessee and, fortunately for me, Ellington's executive secretary was Bo Roberts, who was a good friend of the family and had been a neighbor when he was editor of The Sevier County News Record, now The Mountain Press. So we worked very well together and I think together helped accomplish some good things for the state of Tennessee.

Certainly one of the most powerful men in the United States Congress at that time was Joe L. Evins. Mr. Evins was a representative from the 4th Congressional District, a Democrat, and chairman of the subcommittee that appropriated funds for the Appalachian Regional Commission. He was a strong believer in the commission and a very, very astute politician, and he ran that committee with a very tight hand. I enjoyed working with him too.

Of course, Congressman James Quillen was the representative from my district and it was always a pleasure to work with him, as well as John Duncan, who was a member of the House from the Second Congressional District. At that point in time, Bill Brock was still in the House, representing the Third District. However, during that time Bill was elected to the United States Senate, having defeated Senator Albert Gore, Sr. We had a good delegation from Tennessee and I worked well with both Democrats and Republicans.

An interesting event occurred while I was at the Appalachian Regional Commission. President Nixon was looking for a university campus to appear at because campus unrest was very, very bad during that time and there were a lot of demonstrations on campuses. Howard Baker told him he would always be well received at the University of Tennessee in Knoxville, that the Knoxville area was generally very supportive of Nixon. But as it turned out, an even better invitation occurred, because Dr. Billy Graham was holding one of his crusades in Knoxville and was scheduled to speak at Neyland Stadium, the University of Tennessee football stadium in Knoxville. Billy Graham invited Nixon to come to Knoxville and appear with him at the crusade.

As I had mentioned, campus unrest had been pretty tough all through the United States during that particular time and security was very, very tight. Of course, security is always tight when the President of the United States comes, but I think it was particularly tight there and practically every police officer and state trooper in the East Tennessee area was brought in to perform duties in one way or another involving security during this event. The UT stadium was a big stadium even then and was filled to capacity for Dr. Graham. He was certainly a very popular man in the East Tennessee area. A man named Fred Hillis was a state trooper stationed in Sevier County at that time, and Fred was assigned a position in the stadium where it occurred that a small number of demonstrators sought to disrupt the program in the usual way, by hollering and waving banners, and just generally being disruptive. It was a small number and they were brought under control very quickly. After the event was over I was talking to Fred and since I had heard that he was in the area where this happened, I asked him about it.

I said, "Fred, was there ever any danger up there?"

And he said, "Well, there wasn't any danger with those demonstrators. There were just a few of them and we got them under control very quick, but let me tell you something: If those Christians got turned loose then there wouldn't have been anything in the world we could have done to stop it!"

I found it a rather amusing story, and not too long after that I was in the White House for a meeting with Nixon, and I told him that story. Nixon loved it. Howard Baker said that he knew that Nixon repeated that story many, many times after that.

At JBW's swearing in TVA.
Left to right, JBW, Bill Willis, Chili Dean, Dick Freeman

JBW at TVA

Alex Hailey and JBW at TVA

Left to right: JBW, President Ronald Reagan, Marvin Runyan, C, Dean in Oval Office

THE TENNESSEE VALLEY AUTHORITY

I can't say that I really had an early desire or ambition to be a director on the Tennessee Valley Authority. However, in 1984 I was completing my year as president of the Tennessee Bar Association and I had become somewhat burned out in the practice of law. I dearly loved the practice of law and before that time I could never have imagined doing anything else. But in 1984 I began to think about TVA. They were having difficulty in finding a person that was acceptable to go on the TVA board. It was primarily the decision of Senator Howard Baker, who was the majority leader of the United States Senate. A number of names had been suggested. I don't recall the details or problems, but none seemed to have the acceptability that was needed to get the Presidential appointment and confirmation by the United States Senate.

I talked about this problem with Howard Baker. I told Howard that I thought I'd like to be on the board, and I'd like to be considered if he thought it was appropriate. I don't think Howard really thought that I was that interested in going on the board, but as time passed, the politics and difficulties in the board appointment seemed to become more intense and one day Tommy Griscom, Howard's press secretary, called me on the telephone and said, "Are you really interested in appointment to the TVA board? Before you answer, I want to tell you that if you are, you are likely going to be appointed very quickly. Howard has decided that he's going to move on this situation. He's going to put somebody up."

So I said, "Let me think about this." I talked with Patsy and I later called Tommy back and said, "I'm interested in it. I think I'd like to be on the board." Howard recommended me to President Ronald Reagan and in August, 1984, I went on the board. It was interesting that during the appointment process, I went for the required interview at the White House. There had been quite a bit of talk about other people being appointed and people other than Senator Baker had made recommendations, or at least there had been some press that other recommendations were going to be made. At the White House President Reagan told me that whomever Senator Baker wanted was who he was going to appoint. I thought that was a pretty good opportunity for me to get appointed.

The opportunity to serve on an agency that managed a large river system was very appealing to me, due to my love of rivers and, frankly, I saw myself repeating my childhood chores of running up and down the river, only this time it would be the big Tennessee River.

When I got to TVA in August, I found that TVA was a troubled agency. In the late seventies and first two years of the eighties, TVA's residential rates had doubled, reaching about 80 percent of what the national average was at that time. It was the time of the energy crisis of that era and much higher coal prices.

My two colleagues on the board when I arrived were Charles H. (Chili) Dean, who was chairman then, and Richard (Dick) Freeman. I enjoyed serving with both of these men on the board. Chili had been the general manager of the Knoxville Utility Board and was interested in power and knew a lot about the power business. Dick had at one time worked for TVA, but was an attorney by profession and had been in Chicago representing a railroad and came to TVA shortly after Dave Freeman by appointment of President Carter. Bill Willis at that point in time was the general manager of TVA.

Dick Freeman was a very smart man, a very quick study and quick reader. He could read and assimilate a lot of very complicated information, which was a very valuable asset on the TVA board since you were given tons of material to read. Dick was a very strong environmentalist. He believed very strongly in improving environmental quality and he opposed almost anything that he felt would impact the environment.

TVA had been through the large nuclear construction period. At one time it had about 50,000 employees. I spent an awful lot of my time on nuclear power. It was such an important problem in the agency at that time. I found that TVA for some reason had turned away from the river, or at least it seemed to me that there was not the emphasis on the river that there should be. I was amazed to find maps of the valley that were given to the board for various discussions and information sources that didn't have the Tennessee River on them. I suppose this was one of my first direct orders. I said I didn't want to see any more maps of the Tennessee Valley that didn't have the Tennessee River on them. The river itself was just not often a subject for conversation in TVA. Also, it seemed to me that TVA had lost its focus on the river system.

The original vision of Franklin Roosevelt and Senator George Norris was that of an integrated development in the watershed of the Tennessee Valley, and I thought that this was one of the greatest experiments and dreams of mankind. I felt like TVA had enjoyed tremendous success in this endeavor in its early years.

Because of a number of these problems, TVA had lost a lot of credibility with the public. The press treated us a little bit like a wounded animal in the forest; we were down and it was time to pile on. The agency was coming under tremendous criticism. Many people were very critical of what TVA was doing. Of course, we have to remember that people at that particular time were questioning all systems of government and TVA may have served, in some instances, as the whipping boy.

In addition to the other serious problems of the nuclear power system, I thought that TVA needed to do things in a more business-like way, to find a way to revitalize the great heart of the agency which was its resource development program. That's what made TVA unique and what made TVA an example for other nations, especially among the developing nations which constantly sent representatives to TVA to study our plan. When you looked at the tremendous work TVA had done in soil erosion and reforestation, I felt as if we were simply not focusing on these great programs as much as we should. A lot of work was being done at TVA, but in many instances we weren't working together. We weren't working with other agencies to the extent that we should have been, it seemed to me. We weren't working as well with state and local governments as I felt we should have been. I felt as if a focus was needed, and to me that focus could best be brought about by a return to the river system.

I didn't like using the term "reservoirs" to describe our lakes. To me a reservoir was a tank on top of a hill. I didn't like continually saying that the dams were built basically for power production. Yes, indeed, they were built for power, but they provided a good deal more. It seemed to me that we were continually disclaiming responsibility for our own lakes and dams. I felt they were our lakes and we should claim them. We should make these lakes meet the original vision of Roosevelt and Norris: a means of developing the valley and improving the quality of life there. I felt like the Tennessee River was still one of the most important resources that the valley could have, and we needed to work cooperatively with the valley. We could do this, I felt, by turning our attention to the river. For some reason or another I found a lot of resistance to this idea inside TVA.

Lake levels in the valley were a constant source of public concern. Fishermen, boating enthusiasts and people who lived on the lakes were constantly upset when the lakes were drawn down. I didn't think TVA had done a good job of explaining this to the public and I felt we needed to see if we could improve that system. So I started pretty early on with what later became our Lake Improvement Program, and I think this was a very successful program and one that I'm proud of. Some wag once made a statement which I learned to be very true. There are two things you need to do to be a good TVA director: "Lakes up, rates down."

It was an unpopular time to go on the TVA board. I worked very hard just getting up to speed, to know what was going on in the power system and understand the non-power program, and especially to learn as much as I could about the river. I recall having to learn about a billion dollars. As a small-town lawyer, I had never had to consider a billion of anything. It was just simply an amount that I didn't really grasp, and I recall finding out that I was mistakenly thinking that a billion was a hundred million. When I found out finally that a billion was a thousand million, I really appreciated Senator Everett Dirksen's remarks on the floor of the Senate when he was talking about the billions that the government spends. He said, "Mr. President, a billion here and a billion there and pretty soon you're talking about real money."

Well, I found that to be true. A billion really is a thousand million, and I finally learned to assimilate in my mind that very, very important fact.

As I said, it was an unpopular time. I made a lot of speeches when I first went to TVA. Any new director is invited to speak a lot. People all over the valley want to get acquainted with him. I got a lot of mileage out of a story I used a lot, commenting on the unpopularity of TVA at the time. The story

I told went like this.

I said that when I practiced law in Sevierville, my home town, that really I was a very popular man. People liked me. I had grown up there and I knew a lot of people. When I walked down the street, people would holler at me, "Hi, Johnny!" And they would wave at me and I would wave back, and I was generally popular. But I said that after I came to TVA and got on the board, I was not as popular, it seemed to me. When I saw people, some would still wave, but they never held up as many fingers.

This story got a lot of laughs, especially with public officials of the time. Many had suffered from the same problems.

Another story which I often repeated and enjoyed hearing myself, was a story about David E. Lilienthal, who was on the first board of the TVA, and later, of course, was chairman of TVA. The story is that Lilienthal was in a car with some other TVA officials driving along the Tennessee River, probably looking for places to build dams. They were on a road that went into the river where a ferry served crossing the river. It was twilight and the ferry boat was not there, and for some reason the driver of the car accidentally drove off the road into the river. The occupants of the car got out as best they could. No one was injured, but they were certainly wet. Lilienthal and his wet friends walked up to the ferry master's house and knocked on the door. The master was not there, but his wife came to the door and Lilienthal said, "Lady, you ought to put a sign up here telling people about the river."

To which the woman replied, "My God, mister, if you can't see the river, how do you expect to see a sign?"

When we talk about the Tennessee River and river management and the issues that are involved in river management today, it's helpful to understand just a little bit about the Tennessee River, the tributaries and the dams that we have built there. The Tennessee River and its tributaries are part of a river and lake system that includes more than forty constructed lakes connected by stretches of the Tennessee River. The river system includes 600,000 acres of lake surface and more than 11,000 miles of shoreline.

TVA built most of these forty dams. Some were bought and TVA operates others that do not belong to the Tennessee Valley Authority but still contribute to our integrated water control system. The Tennessee River is the only major river system in the country operated by a single agency with responsibility for unified resource development. I found this to be a very important factor and one that made TVA more unique than you might first realize. TVA operates the river for navigation, flood control and power production. This is what was set out in the act that created TVA. Yet, today TVA faces problems never contemplated when the agency was first created. At the dawn of the twenty-first century, we are faced with increasing conflicts over the use of lakes and rivers. The range and complexity of issues are greater than ever before. So it's very important to make sure that our approach to river management keeps pace with the responsibility and what the public needs are today.

The very earliest settlers of the Tennessee Valley were certainly concerned about water quality. As a matter of fact, good, clear, crystal springs were one of the great things that were looked for when a settler first decided where to build his log cabin to try to raise his family. Clean and clear water was important even in those days. But while people recognized poor water quality when TVA was first created, they didn't worry about a number of things we know to be concerned about today. For example, they probably didn't worry a lot about low dissolved oxygen or PCBs or any of the thousands of chemical pollutants than had not yet found their way into the waterways. It's not hard to think of a host of other problems that were non-issues in this early era of the 1930s. Those concerns include wastewater management, groundwater protection, drought, wetland protection, recreation, tourism, property values along the lakes, and thermal pollution from power plant cooling.

All of us are aware of some of the issues that are involved in population growth and urban development, and most of us certainly realize the increase that population growth causes in sources of pollution. Twelve sewage treatment plants discharge almost fifty million gallons of treated sewage into the Fort Loudon reservoir every day. This drains Knox and Blount Counties and parts of Loudon County down to the Fort Loudon dam. The bacterial concentrations in urban runoff entering Fort Loudon are much higher than in the sewage treatment discharges, however, and the oxygen demand from Second Creek alone, which drains about ten percent of Knoxville, is greater than the oxygen demand of the combining discharges of all four Knoxville sewage treatment plants. Keep in mind that dissolved oxygen in the river is necessary for the water to clean itself and to handle and manage whatever pollutants get into the water. You will agree that water sports and recreational activities on the Tennessee River today are many times what they were when TVA was first created, and even though water sports recreation was a factor in those days, it is a much more serious factor today and involves more people and a considerable amount of money that comes into the economic development of the area that would otherwise not occur without this valuable asset of the Tennessee River. An example is Melton Hill Lake. A couple of hundred rowers are using Melton Hill for their version of spring training. Team members from Syracuse, Dartmouth, Michigan and many other schools are joining students from the University of Tennessee and other schools in this region, because Melton Hill is considered one of the best rowing sites in the East. Many regattas are held there each year.

In the early days of TVA, power production was an important matter and production of hydroelectric power was one of the primary reasons for the development of TVA dams. But today at TVA we have another power system which requires an awful lot of water and has an impact on our lakes that was unheard of at the time TVA was organized. TVA's nuclear power represents a safe, clean, and vitally important part of our power system. When both reactors are running at Sequoyah Nuclear Plant on the Chickamauga Reservoir just north of Chattanooga, they require 1,600 million gallons of cooling water a day. For that reason you see the big cooling towers near nuclear plants where the water is cooled before it can be safely discharged back into the river.

TVA today deals with a number of new forms of water-based industries. For example, a fledging commercial mussel industry on the Kentucky Reservoir handles over $16 million worth of mussel shells each year. Then there is the issue of aquatic weeds. About fifty thousand acres of mainstream TVA reservoirs are infested with these weeds. Many fish and anglers like that, but boaters and residents do not. So it is a very important issue and one that we have to deal with regularly.

I had not been at TVA very long before I realized that as competing demands on the river system grow, we need a better way to resolve conflicts over the use of this important resource. We need a new way of doing business when it comes to river basin management. It must be broad in scope and address all the needs and uses of the river. It should help build consensus among local, state and private interests, and practices must meet expected performance. One of the big problems that faces water quality today all over the United States and indeed all over the world is non-point source pollution, a problem that affects two-thirds of this nation's watersheds and contributes an estimated eighty percent of the pollutants that enter the Tennessee River. Many pollutants come from literally thousands of sources up and down the valley, such as landfills, applications of fertilizer and pesticides, underground storage tanks, accidental spills, septic tanks, abandoned land mines, urban runoff and the millions of motor vehicles on our highways that cause pollution which eventually gets into our streams and into our water. The waste from the many herds of dairy and beef cattle that live in the valley often runs off into the river and is a source of non-point pollution. Many farmers are working today with TVA and the soil conservation people and other state and federal agencies to address this problem and big improvements are being made. But the problem is large. There are eighty-five thousand livestock farms in the TVA watershed, and 4.7 million head of cattle. Their waste is equal to the untreated sewage of 47 million people, and that is more than six times the population of the Tennessee Valley. So you can see what an incredible amount of labor and money is involved in taking care of a problem such as this.

It was my opinion that we needed very badly to develop a better way to work with interested citizens, to network with these citizens, to find out what was on their minds and get input from them. We needed a structure of achieving consensus with them. We also needed a system for measuring our progress and we needed a means of assuring that the best management practices were designed and operated to meet these high standards. I felt that we needed very badly a user-oriented performance indicator for general river management. Appropriate performance indicators could allow both river managers and users to identify who has the responsibility for various activities on the river and how well they are performing their jobs. That way they can see how well a project is working, where the weaknesses are, and what needs attention. Performance indicators could also help river managers better match their programs to the needs of the rivers. The indicators need to be broad and relate to every aspect of our lives on the river. These include home and community, environment, public health, economic satisfaction, leisure time, safety, education, and cultural development transportation.

I was at that time serving on the board of the Institute of Nuclear Power Operators headquartered in Atlanta. Utilities that had nuclear plants had formed the institutes after the Three Mile Island accident to improve and monitor nuclear safety in nuclear plants in the United States. There had never before been a TVA board member on the INPO board. INPO had developed performance indicators to evaluate nuclear plants. I saw these as very effective because they gave you an opportunity to look at trends and see where you were improving and in what areas you had problems, and I felt we could do that with TVA. I was very happy that we did later develop the River Pulse publication, which I think was a big improvement in getting this kind of information to the public.

One of the primary reasons for enacting the Tennessee Valley Authority was to improve the social and economic development of the valley by improving the navigability of the Tennessee River. The Tennessee River waterway consists of 650 miles of main channel and 150 miles of secondary channels, which are part of the nation's 10,000 miles of interconnected, inland waterways. The main channel connects Paducah, Kentucky, with Knoxville, Tennessee, and also connects the Tennessee-Tombigbee Waterway to a direct route to Gulf Coast ports. Commercial navigation also extends sixty-one miles up the Clinch River to Clinton, Tennessee; nineteen miles up the Little Tennessee to Vonore, and twenty-two miles up the Hiwassee River to Calhoun, Tennessee.

The Tennessee River has ten dams with locks on the main channel and an additional dam with locks at Melton Hill. Four have main auxiliary locks and one, Nickajack, has the underwater portion of a new lock completed. Six of these dams have 110-by-600-foot locks, with a new lock at Pickwick measuring 110 by 1,000 feet. The 110-by-600-foot lock is considered a standard for modern barge traffic. The practical lock capacity of a 110-by-600-foot lock varies between approximately 33 and 40 million tons. All the dams of the middle and lower sections of the waterway have these big locks. Three dams, Chickamauga, Watts Bar and Fort Loudon, have one 60-by-360-foot lock. These smaller locks north of Chattanooga need to be replaced and enlarged as soon as possible if we are to keep good navigation on the Tennessee River.

Many people don't understand the importance of river navigation because they occasionally see a tow-boat pushing a number of barges on the river and that may be all they know. But when you consider that only one of those barges (and a tow boat will often push several, sometimes fifteen or twenty) can transport what it takes sixty tractor trailer rigs to haul on the highway or fifteen rail cars by train. So when you're moving a lot of heavy cargo, river transportation is very important to the economic development of the valley, and especially to the East Tennessee section.

After a lot of work and many, many hours of time put in by a number of capable people on the TVA staff, I was able to bring to the board in February 1990, TVA's Lake Improvement Plan. This was adopted by the board and it represented the most comprehensive change ever in the way TVA operates the Tennessee River System, the sixth-largest river system in the United States. This plan was the result of a thorough public review of operating priorities for the river system. It took about three years to develop and it cost $4 million (about half the time and a tenth of the cost of a comparable FERC relicensing process, FERC being the Federal Environmental Regulatory Commission). As a result of this study, TVA increased minimum flows at all dams across the system. In other words, we very seldom cut the water off at any dam. We continued a minimum flow through the dam because we learned in this study how important a minimum flow is to water quality.

We began aeration improvement to at least six dams to improve dissolved oxygen in tail waters, and, very, very important to residents, fishermen and boaters, we improved summer levels for recreation on ten tributary lakes. We found out we could draw the lakes down in the fall instead of the early summer as we had been doing, which allowed the lakes to stay up at the maximum level for the summer period, which of course is the most important time for recreation on the lakes. These changes improved conditions for aquatic life in over 300 river miles and improved recreation and economic development in the tributary areas without affecting the level of benefits traditionally provided to navigational interests and power consumers.

TVA had hundreds of staff people working on this problem and I can't compliment those people enough on the quality and dedication they gave to the job. I hesitate to mention names, but I feel like I must. Christopher D. Ungate was a leader in this effort and is, in my opinion, one of the truly great experts on lake and water management in the country. Stephen D. Derby, Rene Hurst, Doug Walters and many others worked on this very important project. But these people took the leadership and certainly deserve any credit.

I have to rank TVA's Lake Improvement Plan as one of the most rewarding contributions I was able to participate in during my time on the board. I felt very strongly about this and I felt very proud to have had any part in the development of this plan and the improvements that were made by the plan in the way TVA operates the river system.

Figure 4
DIAGRAM OF TVA WATER CONTROL SYSTEM

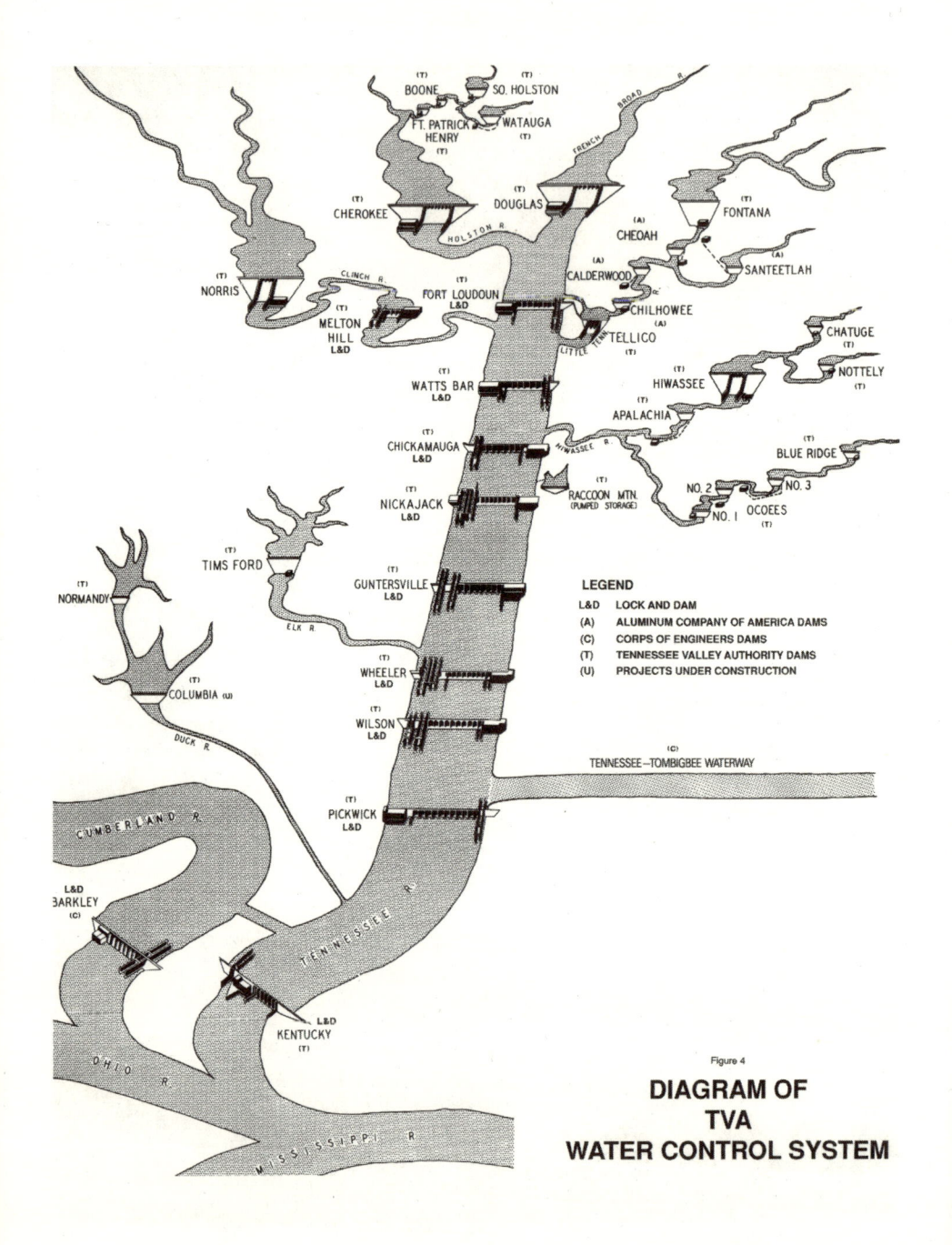

JBW at the controls in the Pilot House of the Maggie B

Scene of the Maggie B. on the TVA inspection trip on the Tennessee River meeting a large tow upbound.

VOYAGE FOR THE VALLEY

When I came to TVA I had an opportunity to learn a lot about the Tennessee River, and because of my love for rivers in general, I took every opportunity that came my way to get better acquainted with the big Tennessee River. TVA has a lot of very fine staff people who have various expertise in matters relating to the river. There are a lot of experts in water quality, fish biology, and flood control. Others are expert in navigation and recreational land management along the river, as well as economic development. So TVA was the ideal place to learn about the river.

Of course, I had an interest in the river before I came to TVA. In 1976, when I headed up the Sevier County Bicentennial Project of the Smoky Mountain Queen, we built a flatboat and left Sevier County on the Little Pigeon River, travelling into the French Broad, then into the Tennessee, the Ohio and the Mississippi, and on to New Orleans. People who live on or near the river or make their living from the river are interesting people, and I had an opportunity to meet a lot of people like that while I was at TVA. There were riverboat pilots, lock and dam operators, sand and gravel operators, commercial fishermen, musselers, tow and barge company officials, port authority executives, people who owned and operated the marinas and boat docks, riverfront development people, and people who just wanted to have a home or vacation home on the river. So many people use the river for recreation. They come for boating, fishing and sightseeing. They include yacht club officials and people who like to camp along the river. A number of other people work in a field that touches the river, such as corporate officials from paper, chemical, energy, railroad, trucking, construction and agribusiness industries. Other people have environmental interests. Engineers and planners have work that touches the river, and an awful lot of decision makers need to know more about the river because they're making decisions in their city or county governments, state legislatures or federal agencies, that touch on the river and impact the river. I became concerned that a lot of people didn't know as much about the river as I thought they needed to know. Many really didn't understand the river. Some people did not even view it as an asset. It was something to cross to get where you were going, and sometimes the bridges weren't in the right place and were inconvenient. The river would sometimes flood and cause damage to property, so some people had a real fear of the river. So I became aware that I needed to find some way to give this widely varied group of people a better understanding and appreciation of the river, so that when they made decisions that impacted the river they were aware of that impact. They also needed to be aware of the advantages of the river, the opportunities that the river presents.

Early on I started talking about some sort of river inspection trip. I wanted to see if there was some way I could get these people on the river. I knew that if they saw the river only from highways and banks, they wouldn't get the perspective that is achieved when you are actually on the river. I had a number of experiences which made me feel even more strongly about this matter. On more than one occasion, when some reporter would write a news article about the river, I would feel that he or she didn't understand about the river and I would invite that person to come on the river with me and look it over. Almost without fail, when I did this that person would come away with a totally different perspective. So I talked to people in TVA about doing a river inspection, a river trip. I wanted to be the first TVA director to travel and inspect the entire length of the Tennessee River.

A number of people at TVA encouraged me to do this, although others didn't think it was too good an idea. One of the people who encouraged me was Craven Crowell, who has since become chairman of the TVA board, but at that time headed up our communications and public relations department. Craven was a former media person at the Nashville Tennessean, and he had a lot of public relations experience. He thought the river inspection trip was a good idea and thought it could be a valuable tool in public relations for the river and for TVA in general. I talked a lot to Bill Willis, general manager of TVA, about a river inspection trip and Bill encouraged me to go ahead with it, so I formed a working committee that began to consider how a river inspection trip could be conducted.

TVA had a number of towboats, probably fifteen or more. Most of these stayed near the coal-fired plants on the river because coal was delivered to the plants by barge and towboats were needed to move the barges around to where they could unload their coal and then get them back out where the other towboats could pick them up and take them back to use again. TVA also had the Pellissippee, which stayed on the river almost continuously servicing the navigation aides, the buoys, signs and markers on the river banks, which TVA had responsibility for on the Tennessee. The Corps of Engineers generally performs this function on the inland navigation streams.

TVA's largest towboat at the time was the Maggie B. I later renamed the Maggie B in honor of TVA's chairman, Red Wagner, who was a man who came up through TVA and river work and was a lover of the river. I thought it was fitting, after Red died, that the Maggie B be named the Red Wagner. I was proud to get that done. The Maggie B at that time was used up and down the Tennessee, generally to haul heavy equipment, big cranes and bulldozers and all kinds of heavy equipment that was needed in TVA construction or work on coal fired plants, nuclear plants or other projects. So it stayed on the river and pushed a number of barges. TVA had a large number of big steel barges used to haul cargo up and down the river. But none of these boats could carry the number of people that I wanted to have with me, getting on and off at various locations to learn about the river. Bill Willis, who was a civil engineer, came up with a plan that we thought would work. I didn't want the trip to cost any more than necessary. We were very conscious of what the trip would cost because we knew we were talking about some real money. But Bill came up with the idea of taking one of the TVA barges, just a flat steel barge, and putting on it one of TVA's many mobile offices. These structures look and are built just like mobile homes, except they are configured on the inside for office use or large working areas. We found one that had two rooms, one very small with bath facilities at one end, and a large open room. When we placed this on the barge it left about a four-foot walkway on each side and room in front and back. This made a nice facility to protect people from the weather when necessary and we could have meetings and informative lectures in the building as well. We repainted and cleaned up the Maggie B to push the barge. The Maggie B was piloted by TVA river boat captain John Howlett, who proved to be a tremendous asset on the entire trip. He was a very fine river boat captain, a second generation captain in his family. He lived in Alabama, but loved the river and knew every crook, turn and buoy on the Tennessee River, and was an expert pilot. John also knew a lot of river lore and stories and we got to be good friends, and I've always valued my friendship with him.

John's crew, Jerry Best and Daniel Garry, kept the Maggie B clean and ready to go in good working condition. They were always willing to do anything we needed to do to make the trip a success. Buddy Staniford was head of the equipment division that was in charge of all the TVA boats, and he and his people cooperated in the project as well.

A number of people were extremely important to the success of the river trip. One whom I worked with in so many other ways throughout my time at TVA was then Lt. Charles Smith, now a commander, with TVA Public Safety (now TVA Police). Charles Smith was a very fine public safety officer, a second generation at TVA. His father had been a TVA public safety officer as well. Charles married a Sevier County girl, Ersa Rae Noland, whose father had been high sheriff of Sevier County. Charles was a friend and an asset and a help to me, not only on the river trip, but all the time that I was at TVA.

Another group of people who performed a tremendous service was the Tennessee Valley Bicentennial Volunteers. This group had been formed back in the 1976 Bicentennial year to do a lot of promotion and historical work on TVA. They had such a good organization that they kept the group intact. These people were TVA retirees and they did a fantastic job of helping us along the trip. We didn't travel at night, so we picked up people such as local officials, mayors, county and city officials and industry leaders in the morning, and they would ride down that day maybe until noon when they would get off the boat and we would pick up another group. We had to have vans to transport people getting off the boat back to their vehicles they had left behind. The TVA Bicentennial Volunteers, with TVA vans, performed this duty and we hosted over a thousand people on the boat for half- or full-day trips. The volunteers also helped with food and refreshments that had to be served, including lunch almost every day. The logistics of getting supplies and people on and off the tow boat was a big job. Russ Allen was director of the volunteers and headed up a group which included James L.

and Faye Thompson of Signal Mountain, Tennessee; Clarence and Juanita Hill of Kingston; Glen and Joyce Moultrie of Chattanooga and John Shearon of Sheffield, Alabama.

Of course, one person that I absolutely could not have done without was Sandy McMahan, now Thompson. Sandy really looked after every detail in the trip. She helped me organize and manage invitation lists, she looked after logistics, she made sure that whatever we needed was on board and ready when we needed it, and she acted as our informal hostess for the entire trip. Sandy also managed Captain Howlett and his crew, the BVI volunteers and did just a fantastic job. As I said, the logistics of this trip were considerable.

We wanted to keep a record of the trip, and I was very fortunate to have the assistance of Dr. Phillip J. Mummert, who worked with me from the beginning on the trip. Phil kept a log and documented where we were going and what time we got there and who was there. He helped pull the trip together and helped bring on the TVA experts who came on board the ship and, as we went down the river, would talk about various aspects of water quality, fish, or soil bank erosion. When we would pass a steam plant, someone would be on board who could answer questions about that facility and tell how it worked and operated. Therefore, the people who came on board for a portion of the trip got a pretty good education and came away with a good knowledge of TVA in general, as well as the river.

On Monday, June 4, 1990, at 9 a.m. Eastern Daylight Time, all my planning and the hard work of so many people came to fruition when we started downbound on our river inspection trip. We left the Forks of the River, which is where the French Broad and Holston Rivers come together and the Tennessee begins. We had already picked up at Knoxville Dock our guests for the day.

We had a cordless microphone and sound system aboard the Maggie B so that anyone at any time could describe points of interest and provide information or color commentary along the way and be heard by the passengers.

Not many people think of Knoxville as a gateway, but at this point you are at the water gateway to the entire world. From here you can go anywhere in the world that can be served by water. It is approximately 1,500 water miles to the Gulf of Mexico via the Mississippi River, which is about an eighteen day trip. It's about half that distance via the Tennessee-Tombigbee Waterway. The Tennessee-Tombigbee made water transportation from Knoxville, Tennessee, just half the distance and time it had been prior to construction. In any event, from the Forks of the River, the headwaters of the Tennessee River, it's all downbound and we were under way.

As we passed downtown Knoxville and the University of Tennessee I was reminded of the Vol Navy, that large flotilla of yachts and boats that come to all UT home football games. The flotilla was getting to be well-known all over the country at that time.

Residential homes lined the waterway downstream from Knoxville and we were fortunate to have on board my friend, area auctioneer Sam Furrow, who turned out to be the primary commentator on the barge, pointing out the various residences along the way and citing some interesting real estate facts and figures. Eighty percent of Fort Loudon Reservoir's shore is in private lands. This is quite typical of reservoirs on the Tennessee River, most of which have at least fifty percent public shorelands.

We were under way fifty miles that first day. We generally averaged about that or a little more on the entire trip.

On the second day of the trip we locked through Fort Loudon and entered the Watts Bar Lake. Watts Bar is one of the most beautiful lakes in the entire system. An important part of TVA history is here as well. The lock and dam would celebrate their fiftieth birthday in just two years. The electricity produced by this hydroelectric facility amounted to almost $50 million in power revenues. The coal plant here was the first plant in the TVA system. While it is no longer operating, it is affectionately known as "The Academy," for one of its hidden contributions was its use to train those that went on to manage and operate the other eleven coal-fired plants in the TVA system.

When Watts Bar Lock was completed in 1942, the size of barges used on the river was quite small compared to today's vessels. The old barges could conveniently fit in the Watts Bar Lock, but today we have the "jumbo sized" barges which provide greater efficiency in handling cargo. But the Watts Bar Lock and other small ones of that vintage were not built for the bigger barges and they cause slowdowns in river traffic. Only one jumbo barge can lock through at a time, while the newer, bigger locks downstream from Chattanooga can handle eight barges at a time. The big barges are one hundred and ninety-five feet to two hundred feet long and thirty-five feet wide, and they can carry approximately fifteen hundred tons of a commodity. Compare this with the one hundred tons that can be carried by a coal car on a railroad. One jumbo barge can haul what fifteen railroad cars can carry.

At this site also is Watts Bar Nuclear Plant. John Scalice, its manager, came on board to explain a little bit about nuclear power to our guests and answer questions about Watts Bar. He captured our attention by showing us a little cylinder about a half-inch long and one-quarter inch in diameter. It was a simulated uranium pellet made out of rubber. It was very small, but it made a big point, for the uranium pellet is equivalent to the energy produced by seventeen hundred and eighty pounds of coal or nearly a hundred and fifty gallons of oil. Millions of fuel pellets would be used in plants like Watts Bar. They would produce electricity to serve the needs of seven hundred and fifty thousand people.

We passed many historical sites on Watts Bar. One was the site of Hiwassee Garrison, where the Cherokee Indians were kept prior to their removal via the "Trail of Tears" in the 19th century. Hiwassee Island was occupied in prehistoric times and later by the Creek Indians until early in the 18th century, and then Chief John Jolly and his band of Cherokees. At Hiwassee Island the Hiwassee River joins the Tennessee. The water that flows into the Tennessee there has already accomplished a lot of work. It has served the needs of communities, been a source of recreation in several mountain reservoirs, and helped produce electricity at five TVA dams in North Carolina and Georgia. It has also carried a lot of what was once whitewater, which rafters and canoe enthusiasts on the Ocoee enjoyed.

Day three we passed Sequoyah Nuclear Plant and TVA's Chief Nuclear Officer Oliver Kingsley came on board the Maggie B to tell us some more about nuclear power, particularly at Sequoyah. While we passed the plant on June 6, Unit One was coming up slowly in power following a fueling outage. Unit Two was near full power, meaning it would be a source of more than eleven hundred megawatts of electricity on this day. At that time the TVA system was expected to provide over seventeen thousand megawatts for the entire system. When both units are at full power they generate more electricity than can be produced by all the hydropower units in the nine dams on the Tennessee River.

Sequoyah uses one million gallons of water every minute. River water flows past the site at an annual average rate of fourteen million gallons per minute, so one-fourteenth of the river's water is used to condense the steam after it has done its work in producing electricity. The water is not consumed. Once it has served its purpose, it is safely returned to the river at an average temperature about two degrees higher than when it was withdrawn.

We then entered Hamilton County and were near the City of Chattanooga, which of course has tremendous recreation boat usage. This, at certain times of the year, places a significant demand on Chickamauga Lock. The lock is one of the small locks like the Watts Bar and Fort Loudon locks. The other locks downstream are all larger. The traffic demands and lock size at Chickamauga combine to form a real bottleneck that has meant an average six-hour wait for tows processing through. There have been instances where large tows with up to fifteen barges have taken more than twenty hours to lock through. This is something that needs to be addressed, and I hope that very soon Congress will appropriate enough money to enlarge this lock, and eventually Watts Bar and Fort Loudon too.

Chattanooga has really done a lot in renovating its waterfront, making a tremendous asset out of the Tennessee River which flows through the city. So much of it is really beautiful country and the Tennessee Aquarium at Chattanooga has made a significant improvement in environmental education along the river and indeed in freshwater rivers throughout the entire world. This thirty-million dollar project was designed to attract visitors and tourists to the city and also to stimulate further planned, mixed-use development adjacent to the aquarium site, including offices, hotels, specialty shops, eating places and museums.

We soon navigated the circumference of Moccasin Bend, a thousand-acre parcel of land that lies between Lookout Mountain to the west and a portion of Chattanooga's old and busy industrial waterfront, full of history from the Civil War and other events in the surrounding area. We then entered the Tennessee River Gorge, sometimes called the Grand Canyon of the Tennessee. Lookout Mountain was to our backs, Signal Mountain to our right front and Raccoon Mountain to our left. Into the gorge we followed a path of water that has seen so much history and has been the source of Indian tales and folk stories, real and imagined. Generations of travelers attempted to ply this thirty-mile stretch. Many never made it because the waters and surroundings were so unfriendly. The names that were given to the various locations along this stretch of the river that we navigated so easily today stimulate the imagination about what the river must have been like early. There are Tumbling Shoals, the Suck, Suck Shoals, The Pot, The Skillet, and the Pan. The deepest part of the Tennessee River here is over a thousand feet. There is incredible scenery.

About ten miles into the gorge the Maggie B docked at Raccoon Mountain. This unique facility serves a very important purpose in the generation of hydroelectric power. Water is pumped out of the Tennessee River through a thirty-five-foot diameter pipe to the top of Raccoon Mountain, where it is stored in a man-made lake. When peak loads demand increased power the water is sent back down through the same pipe, generating electricity in the generators as it goes along. This is an expensive way to generate power and in ordinary times would not be economical. But we use it for peak shaving time and it serves a very useful purpose that well justifies the cost of building and operating the Raccoon Mountain Pump Storage System.

We were soon into Gunnersville Lake, a very unusual lake. Aquatic weeds have become a big problem here. This lake is the most shallow lake in the TVA system, but also has tremendous boat traffic. Gunnersville doesn't get any deeper than twenty feet, except in the navigation channel. This means that it has more sediment per volume of water, more wind mixing of the lake water and large shell areas where it is easy for rooted and floating plants to grow.

At Gunnersville Dam we locked through for the fifth time on the trip. We slowly coasted into the lock chamber, this one big enough to handle six jumbo barges at a time. As we entered Wheeler Reservoir the river continued on a relatively straight and narrow course. This first section of Wheeler was riverine, almost a natural river. We passed the City of Decatur, a great river town on the Tennessee River, that has enjoyed a lot of river transportation and industry that uses the river as well as recreational activity along the river.

We passed Brown's Ferry Nuclear Plant, TVA's first nuclear plant, which consists of three boiling-water reactors. A lot of trouble has happened to Brown's Ferry and it has been expensive to refurbish this plant and bring it up to the safety requirements that exist today. However, Brown's Ferry is still a bargain in the generation of nuclear power and for the ratepayers of the Tennessee Valley.

Larry Clark, TVA's manager of reservoir water quality, explained to our guests on board the status of water quality on Wheeler Lake. He said that the water quality in Wheeler was very good and suitable for body contact and recreation. The fish, however, were contaminated with DDTs, PCBs and dioxin. DDT levels were declining due to remedial action begun in 1988. The source of the PCBs is not known and dioxin levels that come from the bleached craft paper mill effluent were expected to recede because of changes that were being made at the paper mill near Cortland that would reduce chlorine bleaching at the pulp mill. The runoff of fertilizers, pesticides and sediments were of concern due to the intensive row cropping and livestock production that occurred in the watershed, some of the most intensive in the state of Alabama. The Wheeler drainage area includes several counties that rank high in Alabama in the number of dairy and beef cattle, hogs and pigs, broiler chickens, and egg production. Water pollution can result from the lack of animal waste management facilities or to inadequate operation of existing facilities. Area groups and residents are concerned about all the debris that gets into the river and then washes near shore and is deposited along the banks. Rotting logs and limbs that fall into the river help trap other debris from trash that is thrown into the river by uncaring, non-thinking people. All of the different kinds of pollution have a cumulative effect on the various uses of the lake, especially as a water supply, home for aquatic life and recreational facility. We all have a role in keeping the river clean and all sources of pollution are part of the problem, so we must all work together to solve it. Continued cooperation in monitoring and measuring our progress is very important.

This nearly level to rolling land is used for cotton, soybean and pasture production. At this point on the river the two leading cotton producing counties in the state were on either side. Limestone County on the north bank ranked first and Lawrence County on the south bank ranked second among all counties in Alabama in the production of cotton. The soil is good cotton soil, well drained but capable of holding moisture through dry periods. Large cotton farmers own land along the river.

We were about to enter one of the most historic stretches of the Tennessee River, a part of the river that has frustrated engineers for a century and river travellers for a much longer time. Some historians say that this impenetrable section of the river had more to do with the outcome of the Civil War that is usually credited. Under us near the mouth of the Elk River was the beginning of what used to be a famous river hazard, the Great Mussel Shoals. This is where the old river began its three-and-a-half-foot per mile drop for the next thirty-five miles. In its path was a series of four rocky obstructions, Elk River Shoals, Big Mussel Shoals, Little Mussel Shoals, and the Colbert Shoals. These made year-round navigation impossible, and navigation those few times of the year when conditions were "good" nearly impossible. But on this day all those hazards were beneath us, unseen memories and near the Elk River confluence we were met by a fifteen-barge tow, unaware of the past, easily hauling coal upstream. Only the passing boats churned the calm waters of the river lake.

We were then approaching Wheeler Dam and river traffic was increasing. We were seeing more and more tows with barges. Many of these were called hopper barges, probably loaded with grain. A high proportion of the total tonnage on Wheeler Reservoir was grain and grain products, coal and coke. Approaching Wheeler Dam the Maggie B overtook another tow barge approaching the dam, whose captains had apparently slowed down so we could lock through first. River boat pilots are indeed courteous and helpful to each other.

Wheeler Dam was the first TVA dam to be built on the Tennessee River. It was begun in 1933 and was completed in October 1936. We entered the big main lock at Wheeler Dam, big enough to accommodate nine jumbo barges. Jim Davis of the Corps of Engineers told us that there were five lock operators who rotated work shifts on the lock. Over thirteen hundred barges locked through Wheeler during the previous year, carrying eight and a half million tons of cargo.

We proceeded on into Wilson Reservoir, the oldest and shortest lake on the main river. The federal government has made important investments in Northern Alabama and has been a big player in the economic development of this area. The long history of efforts to improve navigation in the vicinity of the shoals began in 1820, and include nitrate plants built at Mussel Shoals during World War I and Wilson Dam built to provide power plants when TVA was born in 1943. Perhaps no other predominantly rural part of the country has enjoyed so much federal attention. With TVA came the National Fertilizer Development Complex at Mussel Shoals, Wheeler Dam, Wheeler Wildlife Reservoir and Brown's Ferry Nuclear Plant. The Tennessee-Tombigbee Waterway, completed in 1985, was designed to provide cheaper means of transporting heavy cargo from Southern Appalachian states to the Gulf of Mexico and benefits this part of Alabama as well. All of these major investments are related in some historical or functional way to the river.

The sixth day of our journey began with the Maggie B entering the main lock at Wilson Dam. It was then gradually lowered about ten stories to the Florence Canal and through to Pickwick Lake. All the while an electrical engineer, manager of Wilson Dam Hydroelectric Facility, and TVA employees and tour guides, shared with us a bit of the history and facts about this important part of the river. The U.S. Army Corps of Engineers constructed Wilson Dam, beginning in April of 1918 and completing it in 1924.

The river provides a significant benefit in helping produce electricity at lower costs. The cost of producing electricity by falling water is five to ten times less than by other systems. So hydropower is quite a bargain. The river help keeps the cost of producing power down in other ways as well. Even though the force of falling water turning turbines is the cheapest way to create electrical energy, unfortunately not more than twenty percent of TVA's power is produced from this source. The greatest single source of TVA power is from the combustion of coal, about sixty percent. In fact, coal is relied upon more than any other means to generate electricity in the United States. It is the most abundant fuel resource we have, and even though the Tennessee Valley is blessed with good water and we benefit greatly from it, there is only so much water. Our ability to generate power with it is limited by what Mother Nature provides. But the river helps with the generation of power in another way — getting coal to where it is needed economically. There was some evidence of this a bit further down around the bend of the river. There was no hydroelectric dam in sight, but a major coal-handling terminal came into view. The cost of getting coal from the mine to where it is needed is a major expense to utilities. Because coal is so bulky, because tremendous amounts of it are needed, and because it must come on a relatively uninterrupted basis, the best, most economical way to get it from point A to point B is very carefully considered. Generally, it costs half as much to move coal by barge as it does by rail.

Colbert Fossil Plant is an important part of the TVA power system. It is one of eight coal plants built and put in service during the 1950s by TVA, which today has a total of eleven operating coal plants. When operating at its full load, Colbert consumes more than 12 thousand tons of coal a day, and uses more than eight hundred thousand gallons of water every minute for cooling as it produces electricity. Colbert receives more than three million tons of coal a year. If all that coal could be barged to the plant at once it would require over two thousand barges to haul it. Configured at three abreast, these barges would form a tow nearly twenty-five miles long. The same amount of coal would fill a coal train stretching about 320 miles, or from Chattanooga to Memphis.

The Maggie B approached the dock at Colbert Steam Plant to let those on board disembark and to pick up another group of very special guests who would accompany us on the final leg of this day's trip. These were thirty individuals who made up the top management team at TVA. The highest executives responsible for running our nuclear power program, the power system, the river operations, the fertilizer development center, and the resource development programs came on board, as did people in charge of corporate activities like human resources, general counsel, finance, purchasing, communications, information services and so on. I was glad to welcome on board Marvin Runyan, my colleague and chairman of the board. As far as I know, the TVA Board of Directors had never had a meeting on the river, but we did on this day and I was proud to see this happen because I had been wanting for a long time to get TVA's top executives together on the river. I wanted them to get the feel of a first-hand look at this great resource and I was kind like a little boy in a toy store when I finally had them there on the river, with the opportunity to point out things to them.

Marvin Runyan had not only agreed to my river inspection trip, but he had encouraged me to do so and it was a real education and a privilege for me to work with Marvin Runyan on the TVA board. When he came on board, Chili Dean was still on the board and remained for about a year, but the last year or so of Marvin's term, it was just he and I serving on the TVA board, until later Bill Kennoy came on. But at the time of the trip, the board only had two members. Marvin was a great manager of large corporate structures. He had tremendous experience at Ford Motor Company and with the Nissan plant near Nashville. To me Marvin was the best expert of corporate management that I had ever met and he brought a lot of this expertise to TVA. He and I worked well as a team. Marvin was not skilled in the political process and I was able to make some contributions along those lines. So we worked very well together and I was very proud to work with Marvin as chairman of the TVA board, and I was proud to succeed him as chairman when he went to the U.S. Postal System. His record at the U.S. Postal System certainly proves his ability and talent as a large corporate manager. He has brought the postal system to a profit-making, in-the-black system, which most people thought was impossible.

During the conduct of our board meeting on this day, Bill Willis, our chief operating officer at that time and former general manager of TVA, interrupted the meeting to let us know that the Maggie B had just entered his home state of Mississippi. The state boundary was at Bear Creek and in accordance with waterway protocol, the Alabama flag was lowered and the Mississippi flag raised on the Maggie B.

After our board meeting we saw a very interesting demonstration on the stern of the Maggie B. Al Brown is TVA's aquatic biologist. Together with his assistant, Steve Payne, he set up a demonstration of one of the techniques used to monitor the health of TVA's lakes, including the fish and aquatic life in the water and the water quality. The equipment Al uses in his work is a pickup truck with a camper bed on back, inside of which is a small but well-equipped laboratory. He pulls a trailer with a small fishing boat and the boat contains electrical charge equipment so he can create an electrical charge in the water which stuns the fish within a certain distance. He then very quickly takes the fish to his mobile laboratory on the back of the pickup truck and makes a quick examination of the fish, looking at weight and age and color of the fish and identifying what type of fish he has. Then he dissects the fish and examines the internal organs for any abnormalities. He explained that by doing this he can quickly determine most of the common diseases, such as discolored livers, enlarged spleens and swollen kidneys. From such information he is able to spot trouble spots in the reservoirs. He is not able to tell immediately what causes the problems, but he can identify whether the fish are being stressed by their environment. TVA has learned that these techniques could become very valuable and used around the entire country in assessing water quality. He has learned that biological sampling, not only of the fish, but of other aquatic life (insects, mussels, invertebrates, algae) can tell a great deal about how a very complex system is functioning. TVA conducts its biological monitoring of various aspects on a regular basis.

On the seventh day of our trip we began with a tour of the Yellow Creek Embayment. Major investments for economic development were being made here. Yellow Creek seems to be a good location. The embayment links the Tennessee-Tombigbee Waterway to the south with the Tennessee River. As a result the Tennessee River is connected here with the Gulf of Mexico and a deepwater port at Mobile, Alabama, which is just three hundred miles away.

I had a chance to chat with my friend Don Walden. He joined us that morning. For a number of years I served on the Tennessee-Tombigbee Waterway Authority as a member from Tennessee and worked with Don, the authority's executive director. He, of course, is very knowledgeable about the waterway and was very helpful in telling our guests that day something about the waterway. The waterway is two hundred and thirty-four miles long and generally follows down through Northeast Mississippi and Western Alabama and on the port of Mobile. When the project was built, the major excavation took place to build a channel between Yellow Creek Embayment and the Bay Springs Impoundment about thirty miles to the south of where we were. This was called the Divide Cut. During construction, one hundred and fifty million cubic yards of dirt were moved. Three hundred and fifty million cubic yards were moved for the entire waterway, making it the largest earthmoving project in the world. For comparison, two hundred and ten cubic yards of material were moved to make way for the Panama Canal. The waterway opened in 1985, so we were in the fifth year of operation of the Ten-Tom.

It wasn't long until we moved into the Pickwick Lock at Pickwick Dam, the largest and second busiest on the Tennessee River. The lock was longer than three football fields and could accommodate fifteen jumbo barges at once. At the lock many of our onboard guests from Mississippi departed and others from West Tennessee boarded. Then we were lowered more than fifty feet inside the lock and the gates opened and we entered into Kentucky Lake.

This part of the Tennessee River is quite different from the rest of the lakes we had been in. The Tennessee makes an almost ninety-degree bend to the right and then heads north at this point. This six-mile reach just downstream from Pickwick was one of the nine mussel sanctuaries on the Tennessee River. It provided a distinctly different visual experience from the previous parts of the river. Here the river was narrow and like a river. The high banks contained the river and revealed the effects of serious erosion. These vertical profiles of soil bared to the force of water and waves and river current were in some places twenty feet high. They seemed to shelter fallen tree limbs strewn about at their base. They added a tan and yellowish border to each side of the river and contrasted with the forested slopes of hillsides and bluffs that had risen from the river along Pickwick Lake earlier in the day. On the water we would occasionally see a musseler. Musselers have distinctive and functional boats. Usually they are about sixteen feet long, flat bottomed, with a small air compressor and a wooden frame overhead that holds an electric winch and winch rope. This type of boat is used by someone diving for mussel. Other boats, called Braille boats, could easily be identified by the rows of chains that hung from long wooden bars on each side like a giant jewelry display. These bars would be lowered and dragged slowly along the river bottom in the hopes that the mussels would clamp onto the chains. This part of the river, with its high, eroded banks and mussel boats, seemed foreign to a river traveler who had grown up in East Tennessee. It was definitely a product of the West Tennessee environment. We were in rural West Tennessee.

The soils along this part of the river lie within the Southern Coastal Plain, where sandy, silty deposits were left behind four hundred million years ago when the sea retreated from this area to where the Gulf Coast is today. These soils are very productive and easy to farm, but the same characteristics that make them popular with farmers also cause the soil to erode easily if left unprotected from rainfall. Soil washing away from the high upland in West Tennessee helped make this worse in the thousands of acres of bottomlands, such as these found in Hardin County, Tennessee. This was an area through which the river meandered for the rest of this day's trip. Almost two hundred tons of topsoil per acre was known to wash away from some of the areas west of the river each year. Massive amounts of soil washing into streams filled them with silt and sand. This reduced their capacity to hold water and clogged them, and in turn increased the chance of and expanded the area of flooding. TVA has done a lot of work on soil bank erosion, trying to stabilize the banks along the river, especially in this area. It is very difficult to do and we've yet to come up with a practical plan that is economical enough to work.

Once again we passed an area rich in history as we navigated the old river channel that wound its way northward past Shiloh National Military Park, near places whose names can be found in Civil War histories, such as Pittsburgh Landing, Crump's Landing, Diamond Island. We spent quite some time discussing all the ins and outs of this complex part of the river. Possibly none of us felt that we had resolved anything, or brought anything to a final conclusion, but we had a chance to make all the points that we thought were important to make. I believe that we at least left one another feeling a bit better and more willing to see the other's point of view.

On down the river we came to Clifton, Tennessee, an early river town. It's hard for me to say "down the river" when we were going north. It seems like a mistake. But of course, that's exactly what the Tennessee River does — it does flow north and we were going downriver. There was a similar problem in talking about the banks of the river. We often refer to them as the west bank or east bank or north or south bank, but this is confusing because the river makes so many turns and twists. Old rivers especially frequently literally reverse course away from their general direction. That's why most riverboat people speak of the left bank or the right bank. The right bank is the right bank going downstream, and it's a better way to identify what side of the river you are talking about.

Clifton, Tennessee, is an old historical river town. It has a 1904 bank that is rather unusual. It has all its original features still remaining: the original vault, heavily carved wooden teller windows, marble ledges and tile floors. It's now used as the City Hall. Clifton has one of the four remaining ferry crossings on the Tennessee. The ferry was established in 1818, and was an early pioneer crossing in West Tennessee. Clifton was a prosperous river town at the turn of the century and one of the major points along the river. The home of T. S. Stribling, Pulitzer prize-winning novelist, is located in Clifton. Being at Clifton brought back memories of spending the night there on the Smoky Mountain Queen.

Clifton is at river mile one hundred and fifty-eight. As we continued on around the Clifton Bend, passed Beech Creek Island and then Double Islands, we would occasionally go by a mussler or fisherman or people wading along one of the washed-out shelves next to the bank used as a beach.

During the remaining hours of this eighth day of our trip, most of us were about all talked out. Most of the passengers on the Maggie B were busy watching the river suddenly turn into a broad lake. Between the points where the Duck River merges with the Tennessee and our day's destination at New Johnsonville, ten river miles away, the expanse of water became quite impressive. This final ten-mile stretch provided three disparate but vivid images that I will never forget. There was more than enough for a TVA director to reflect upon. Each in its own way represented the impact of TVA.

There was the great blue heron rookery at Duck River, the aerial power crossing upstream from the U.S. 70 Highway bridge, and the ash disposal ponds of the coal plant. There are over ten thousand acres of managed wetlands on Kentucky Lake. These consist of eight dewatering areas that can be drained or filled at the appropriate times of the year to enhance conditions supportive of wildlife. In fact, earlier we had gone through a ten-mile stretch of two of the areas that adjoin one another. Perryville Dewatering is managed by the Tennessee Wildlife Resources Agency. Immediately downstream from it is the Busseltown Dewatering Area managed by the U.S. Fish and Wildlife Services as part of the Tennessee National Migratory Wildlife Refuge. Now we were approaching the largest of these areas, a twenty-seven-thousand-acre unit managed as a national wildlife refuge, where the Duck River joins the Tennessee. The river makes a ninety-degree jog here before it turns northward. As we followed the channel around the bend, we had a wonderful perspective of the refuge from close up as the channel hugged the shore for several miles.

As day nine of our journey began, we were still on Kentucky Lake and had been for three days. At this point we had traveled over one hundred miles on this lake, which stretches across the entire width of Tennessee from north to south. We would navigate nearly sixty more miles this day.

It was noon when we entered the marina at Paris Landing State Resort. The sun was very hot and we were greeted by Herman Jackson, county executive of Henry County. As we waited to be joined by various Tennessee officials, including members and staff of the state House Committee on Conservation and representatives of the Tennessee Municipal Power Association and the Tennessee Conservation League, I noticed some early clouds beginning to gather high in the sky. Everyone easily gathered and we headed out. We entered the navigation channel and headed downstream. Three miles later we reached the point where the Commonwealth of Kentucky was on our left and the State of Tennessee on the right, forming the notch in the Kentucky-Tennessee state line which runs east-west. More clouds seemed to be forming quite rapidly and it began to look as if we weren't going to make it the whole way from Knoxville to Paducah without some rain. Another several miles, the sky had become very dark in the west and suddenly a slight breeze picked up and intermittent rain drops began to fall. Then the breeze turned to wind and raindrops began to pelt the Maggie B. The captain was eyeing the right bank in search of a safety harbor. The Maggie B began to head toward a small cove on the right side and the rain began to come down harder. It was becoming harder to see. The storm's front edge, marked by whitecaps forming on the lake surface and darkness, moved rapidly across the lake toward us as though it was trying to catch us and beat the Maggie B to shore. Captain Howlett carefully nosed the barge into the cove just as the wind began to whip the boat's flags and awnings. The rain came at us in horizontal sheets and shoreline waves reached several feet as the furious wind forced the thirty-some-odd folks on board inside — that is, except for Bob Koller, our photographer, who stayed outside to catch just a few more shots of the storm's fury. We waited the storm out for twenty minutes. While some of the state officials claimed that it was all created by TVA to demonstrate the use of safety harbors, we all felt content that safety harbors were provided on this river and that the captain knew what he was doing. I was relieved that everyone was safe.

We were in the Land Between the Lakes, or as we know it, LBL. This is a wooded peninsula so named because it is between Lake Barkley, a Corps of Engineers project on the Cumberland River, and Kentucky Lake. The peninsula is about eight miles wide and forty miles long. The area serves as a base for a variety of outdoor recreation, environmental education and resource management activities, with campgrounds, interpretive centers, cooperative research projects, a buffalo range, visitor center and abundant wildlife. While LBL sticks out like a thumb on most maps of this area, from the river a simple beauty, a wooded shoreline, an occasional cove, and the absence of development distinguish it.

On our left we passed one of the major embayments in this area, that of Blood River. Shortly thereafter both the river and our group entered the Commonwealth of Kentucky. Once again, as was our custom, the Tennessee flag came down and the Kentucky flag was two blocked. The LBL staff know how to welcome visitors. That evening they treated us and more than one hundred of our friends from this part of Kentucky to a buffalo tro at Ken

Lake across from where we had put in. By this time the sky had cleared and the sun cast shadows across Kentucky Lake as it set in the west behind us.

LBL is famous for its "buffalo tros." To keep the number of buffalos at a proper number, the number of buffalo must be reduced annually. A small number are slaughtered for the meat. The steaks are very good. The staff will have a buffalo barbecue. They begin by building a fire on the ground out of hickory wood. When the coals are just right, the steaks are "thrown" on the fire to cook. Hence the name, buffalo tro.

Each person that came on this Voyage for the Valley had an interest in the river or they wouldn't have come. Each in his own way appreciated the river and worked to help it, and I gave each person who came on the trip a certificate proclaiming them to be a Friend of the River.

The group that came on board this tenth day was no exception. It was a good mix of people. Dick and Sandy Bell came the whole way from Blairsville, Georgia. Dick had actively participated as a helpful, questioning and concerned citizen throughout TVA's study efforts to improve the operation of the lake system. Initially concerned about summer lake levels in Georgia, he became so fascinated with the whole system that toward the end of the study he wanted to see what the other end of the system looked like. Bob Broadbent, active in public affairs and member of the family that owns and manages a large agricultural operation in Trigg County, was serving as president of the Pennyrile Rural Electric System. Quentis Fuqua, manager of the cooperative where he had been employed for twenty-eight years, also joined us. Carl Hamilton, owner of the Sportsman's Lodge, one of the premier fishing resorts of Kentucky Lake, a member of the LBL Association Board, was also on board. Dr. Dick Marzolf, Commonwealth Professor of Applied Ecosystems Science with the Center for Reservoir Research at Murray State University, was with us. So was Jim Suitor, owner of Holiday Hills Camping Resort on Lake Barkley. Bill Tullar, owner of Patty's 1880 Restaurant in Grand Rivers, joined us on this morning.

Elected officials joined us, including Bryan Blount, mayor of Elton, Kentucky in Todd County; Cecil Mallory, Todd County Judge Executive; and Judy Powell, mayor of Hickman, Kentucky, on the Mississippi. Some were representing elected officials, such as Bob Stowe, Marshall County planner for County Judge Mack Miller; and Gordon Rahn, field representative for Senator Mitch McConnell. Also on board was Dr. Buzz Buffington, who had recently become TVA's director of the Land Between the Lakes. There were, of course, others. I wish I could remember them all.

Several miles downstream from LBL's campground is Barkley Canal, which forms the northern boundary of Land Between the Lakes. I asked Captain John Howlett to take us on a little side trip on the canal as far as Lake Barkley. Then we doubled back to the Tennessee to continue on to Kentucky Dam. It took us only about ten minutes to get to the Cumberland, since the canal was not more than a mile long. This short waterway connects the two lakes to provide continuous bodies of water with nearly a quarter of a million surface acres of water and thirty-five hundred miles of shoreline. We soon stopped at the arrival point for lockage at the Kentucky Dam. Some of our passengers disembarked and others came aboard. Among those coming aboard was Patsy, who joined me for the final leg of the journey.

Kentucky Dam backs up the Tennessee River for one hundred eighty-four miles and creates the lake that we had been on since noon three days before. We were finally in the city limits of Paducah. There are about a dozen barge terminals in the two miles from Cuba Towhead to Broadway Wharf at the mouth of the river. Many key industries were located along this area of the river. Many commodities loaded, including grains, fertilizers, chemicals, sand and gravel, cement and petroleum products. As the Maggie B made her way between the fleeting areas on both sides of the river between Owens Island and the river bank on the city side, the city's floodwall came into view at the top of the bank. The wall is twelve miles long and fifteen feet high. It was built to protect the city following the great flood of 1937. Mayor Gerry Montgomery told me about exciting plans to rejuvenate Paducah's waterfront. The plans included reusing the Waterworks Building as a maritime museum, a waterfront passenger terminal for commercial cruises, and lowering the flood wall to restore visual and psychological links between the city and the river.

The Maggie B entered the busy Ohio River with tow barge traffic moving up and down the river. Then Captain Howlett carefully moved her toward the base of Broadway Wharf. It was 4:30 p.m.

The Friends of Paducah made a special effort to welcome us to their city. Passengers on the Maggie B were met by a group of ambassadors dressed in red and white attire who gave us a warm welcome. It was especially nice of them to come out and greet us.

Our trip was over and I was very pleased with it. It was good to have a satisfactory trip and final day. However, as I looked to the west on down the Ohio where, some forty miles away she joined with the Mississippi, I thought how nice it would have been to continue downbound.

I AM A BAPTIST

The Baptist Church in Sevierville is located two blocks up the street from where I lived at 107 Joy Street. The Sevier County Courthouse is two blocks in the other direction downtown. The Paines and the Waterses were all Baptists. My grandfather, John Mullendore Waters, was a Baptist preacher, and my great-grandfather, Smith Ferguson Paine, was also a Baptist preacher.

Dad said that he decreed that Mother would take care of the religious training for the children and he would handle the political training. Of course, this was perhaps a little bit unfair since Mother was a Democrat and Dad was a Republican, but both were Baptists.

The Baptist church suits me just fine — I like the independence that each Baptist church has, and I also like the independence that each member has.

There are different kinds of Baptist churches. My church, the First Baptist Church of Sevierville, is a member of the Southern Baptist Conference. But our church is autonomous, self-governing. We support the missions of the Southern Baptists and use a lot of the literature they provide for Sunday Schools and other programs. We delegate no power or authority to the Southern Baptist Conference. Most Baptists believe that the power of the Church cannot be delegated. The Church will not empower any person or any body to do anything which will impair its independence.

This independence sometimes gets Baptists a bad "rep" with our fellow Christians in other churches. If a small number of Baptists want to start a Baptist church and practice foot-washing or snake-handling or something else, they can do that and still call themselves Baptists. Most Baptists believe they can read the New Testament and interpret it as they wish. We all believe it is true, but no mortal can bind us to their interpretation unless we agree. Our pastor is our spiritual leader. He reports to no human superior and we can agree or disagree with him if we wish. We have no emblems, other than a simple cross.

Some Baptists are called "Hard Shell Baptists." They have very strong beliefs and opinions. Compromise is not considered a high virtue. Disputes can arise in the church and be difficult to settle. It is not unusual for a faction to leave the church and start a new one. Cousin Tebo was such a Baptist. A dispute had arisen in his church and became very divisive. Finally some of the more reasonable brothers developed a compromise in the interests of harmony. They knew their plan could not succeed unless Cousin Tebo would agree. They visited Cousin Tebo and, after prayer, proposed the plan. Would Cousin Tebo agree? After some thought, Cousin Tebo responded, "No. Before I will agree to that, I will go down here and join the Methodist Church and go to hell!" You can't be a stronger Baptist than that.

To me, faith solves a lot of problems and keeps me from worrying about a lot of questions and theories that many people seem deeply concerned about in religion. I respect those who debate and study and, in general, puzzle over religious doctrines, but to me John 3:16 is enough. It is sufficient.

> For God so loved the world that he gave his only son, that whosoever believes in him should not perish, but have eternal life.

Mark 1, Verse 15, adds,

> Repent and believe.

To me, Christian love is the great duty ordered by Christ. It should make me look leniently on the frailties, mistakes and imperfections of other Christians. Unfortunately, I often fail.

There was a time when the church worried me. As a child I saw very little love and a lot of fire and brimstone. I think this was true not only in our church, but was a sign of those times, particularly following the Great Depression. I was continually taught, it seemed, how bad we were and continually asked to sign a paper that I would not ever engage in a wide variety of sins. These sins varied from those pretty obvious to anyone in the Ten Commandments to a more vast number of sins of omission or commission that the teacher or preacher thought they should impose upon us.

There was one sin I was sure I was not guilty of and had no intention of committing, but I later learned that I had frequently committed, having misunderstood the language. The teacher told us that mixed bathing, that is bathing with a member of the opposite sex, was very bad and should be avoided, and asked us to commit to avoid that sin. I had no intention of taking a bath with a girl, but, alas, I later learned, it meant swimming together, and I had committed this sin every summer.

The church seemed also to be continually asking us to not do a lot of things, and to do a lot of things. We did have what I would now call an escape clause, which I thought was nice even though I didn't exactly understand it at the time and I'm not sure I understand it today. The preacher or leader, for example, would say, "I want everybody to promise to come to Prayer Meeting Wednesday night. Hold up your hand if you'll promise to be here unless providentially hindered." I really wondered what kind of a hindrance qualified as "providentially."

When I was twelve years old we had a revival at First Baptist Church, Sevierville. I am not sure but I believe the preacher's name was Stark. He was a very big man and an excellent speaker. He brought what was to me a new and positive message. On the last Sunday of the revival his sermon was entitled, "The Unforgivable Sin." We could be forgiven of most other sins, but this one was unforgivable. The sin that he referred to was the sin of ingratitude. It struck me as a useless sin, with no reason to be guilty of, but I knew I had been guilty. We were asked to go to someone in the church that we should express gratitude to. Both Dad and Mother were present but not seated together. Dad probably came into church late. I went to both and, of course, the main thrust of the sermon was the sin of ingratitude for Jesus Christ and the Love of God. I became convicted and walked the aisle. There were more than twenty others who also joined the church on that occasion. Later I was baptized. I remember feeling as if I had been sick for a long time, but that I was now well.

Both Johnny B. and Cyndy joined the Baptist Church, and Patsy and I both enjoy and love our church very much. Her family members (the Temples) have all been members of the Baptist Church for many years. Her father, John Ellis Temple, was a deacon in our church. Her brother, Jimmie Temple, and Jimmie's son, James, now serve as deacons.

I must not forget to be grateful and I am indeed grateful. Surely goodness and mercy have followed me all the days of my life.

Left to right: Alexander Waters, Muteyi Waters, Spencer Waters
Our grandsons, downbound at Water's Edge on Little Pigeon River

JBW and Patsy at Water's Edge

Judy and JBW

Cyndy and Shem brought our new grandaughter, four year old Judy, from Kenya, East Africa, just two days before this picture was made. We already love her.

AFTERWORD

Patsy and I still live at Water's Edge in Sevierville, Tennessee. I come to the office every day but I do not do any heavy lifting. My nephew, David Paine Waters, shares the office. David Paine's wife, Tammy, is a teacher in the Sevier County Schools. My brother, David, died August 25, 2000. David's daughter, Susie, and her husband, Walter Davis, live in Knoxville. David's daughter, Louann Dykehouse, lives in Phoenix, Arizona, with her husband, Gary, and sons, Slade and Garret.

My sister, Mary Louise, and brother-in-law, Pete Hailey, live in Sevierville. Pete still practices law. Their daughter, Rachel, and her husband, Charlie Haywood, live in Sevierville. Mary Louise and Pete's son, Ben, and his wife, Helene, live in Knoxville.

The Temple family has scattered. Patsy's brother, Jimmy, and his wife, Marie, are still at Temple's Feed and Seed Store in Sevierville, which everybody calls "The Mill." Their son, James, is also in the business. His wife, Marty, and son, Andrew, live in Oak City on the Temple Farm located there. Patsy's sister, Mary Joyce Hughes, a retired school teacher, lives in Sevierville. Her daughter, Amy Huskins, is a lawyer and lives in Atlanta with her little daughter, Emily. Mary Joyce's son, Matt Hughes, is a soft drink executive. He and his wife, Mary, and their children, Molly and Conner, live in Denver. Patsy's sister, Frankie Cutshaw, lives in a nursing home in Atlanta. Frankie's daughter, Janelle, and Janelle's husband, Art Nevins, have sold their business in Atlanta but still work in the business. Janelle and Art's son, Preston, has graduated from the University of Georgia and their daughter, Whitney, is winning beauty contest in Georgia. Frankie's son, Kenneth Cutshaw, practices law in Atlanta. His wife, Dee, lives in Marietta, Georgia, with their son, Drew, and their adopted Chinese baby daughter, Christina.

Our son, John B. Waters, III, who we call Johhny B, is a lawyer in Knoxville in the Long, Ragsdale and Waters firm. Johnny B's wife, Beth, is busy doing volunteer and church work in the community. Grandsons, Spencer and Alexander, are teenagers.

Our daughter, Cyndy, is a photographer, but Cyndy has become a volunteer missionary in Kenya, Africa. Her husband, Shem, is an African and we now have an adopted African grandson, Muteyi, and a granddaughter, Judy. Cyndy has done some remarkable work in Kenya.

Patsy and I both love and worry about all of our family.